London Eats Out
500 years of capital dining

London Eats Out

500 years of capital dining

Preface by
Loyd Grossman

AUTHORS

Edwina Ehrman
Curator
Costume and Decorative Arts

Hazel Forsyth
Curator
Post-Medieval Collections

Lucy Peltz
Assistant Curator
Paintings, Prints and Drawings

Cathy Ross
Head of Department
Later London History and Collections

MUSEUM OF LONDON

Philip Wilson Publishers

First published in 1999 by
Philip Wilson Publishers Ltd
143–149 Great Portland Street
London W1N 5FB

Distributed in the USA and Canada by
Antique Collectors' Club
91 Market Street Industrial Park
Wappingers' Falls
New York 12590

London Eats Out with SimplyFood.co.uk
An exhibition held at Museum of London
22 October 1999 – 27 February 2000

Exhibition sponsor   Associate sponsors

ISBN   0-904818-93-4 paperback
       0-85667-516-4 hardback

Edited by Moira Johnston
Designed by Museum of London, Design and Exhibitions Department
Designer: Kirsten Laqua
Head of Design and Exhibitions: Moira Gemmill

Printed and bound in Italy by
Società Editoriale Lloyd, Trieste

Cover
Design for the interior of Fischer's Restaurant in Bond Street by Raymond McGrath (1903–77), 1932.

Back Cover
Chips with everything, the façade of a Lyons restaurant at 88 Chancery Lane, 1967.

Frontispiece
1. *A City Chop House* by Thomas Rowlandson, 1805–20.

Contents

Acknowledgements

The authors would like to thank the following for their help and advice.
Simon Blundell, Sally Brooks, Josh Brown, Peter Brown, Ursula Carlyle, Michelle Chambers, John Chase, Corporation of London Record Office, Brian Crowley, Ivan Day, John Deeby QC, Ann Eatwell, Torla Evans, Penelope Fussell, John Freestone, Irene Gilchrist, John Giorgi, Adrian Green, Stephen Green, Guildhall Library, Bart Krieger, Kirsten Laqua, Valerie Mars, Hugo Dunn-Meynell, David Mitchell, Charles Parker, Michael Parkin, Jacqui Pearce, Sara Pennell, Alan Pipe, Nick Redman, Gillian Riley, Adele Schaverien, John Schofield, Susan Scott, Liz Seeber, Roz Sherris, Pauline Siddell, Drew Smith, The Soho Society, John Stevens, Hedley Swain, Richard Stroud, Helen Webb, Robin Weir, Lavinia Wellicome, Alex Werner, David Wickham, Robin Harcourt-Williams, Charles Wright, Peter Urbach. The text covering the last 30 years has drawn on the writings of several restaurant critics, but particularly Fay Maschler and Lindsay Bareham.

Foreword
Simon Thurley

The story of eating out in London holds a mirror to the changing wealth and social style of the city. There is much change; there is much continuity. This book, which has been published to accompany a major exhibition at the Museum of London, traces how the demands of Londoners have been met over the last 500 years, and how their habits have been challenged by outside influences and market forces. It charts the inextricable links between the fortunes of this city and the fortunes of its eateries. It demonstrates how London's infinite capacity for absorption and assimilation, its spirit of entrepreneurialism and its role in the world marketplace have filled Londoners' pockets and stomachs. Eating out is a fundamental part of the social, economic and cultural life of the capital. It has always been important to Londoners, and the city is now regarded as the restaurant capital of the world.

We are grateful to our sponsor SimplyFood.co.uk for helping us to stage the exhibition, and to associate sponsors American Express and Crussh juice bars for their support.

Dr Simon Thurley

Preface

Loyd Grossman

Food nostalgia seduces us into believing that nothing eaten now can possibly taste as good as something eaten in the past. Where are the scones of yesterday, the strawberries of summers past, the burnt sausages of long-remembered picnics? The exception to this wistfulness is the food served in London restaurants. Yet the current rather frenzied celebration of dining out ignores the centuries-old practice of eating in public. It is true that the number and quality of restaurants in London have increased dramatically in the last twenty years, but this book and exhibition show just how rich and varied the dining-out culture of the capital was before Tara Palmer Tomkinson was a glint in some editor's eye.

Conventional restaurant history – like so much writing about food – is relentlessly Francocentric. We are told that the first restaurant was created in Paris in 1765 by Monsieur Boulanger, whose signature dish (as we would call it nowadays) was sheep's feet in white sauce. Part of the motto above Boulanger's door read 'Ego restaurabo vos', or 'I will restore you', and from this sheep's foot beginning sprang both the form and name of the restaurant. While we must admire Boulanger's enterprise, the restaurant was not an invention purely of the age of enlightening; an early lively culture of public eating was based around the tavern, inn and ordinary.

When I arrived in London in 1974 I had no high expectations about the food on offer. I was lucky enough, though, to be introduced immediately to the few glittering exceptions, chief among them being Lacey's (now RIP) in Fitzrovia, the creation of Bill Lacey and his wife, the great food writer Margaret Costa. Sweetings in the City oozed Victorian masculinity but peddled exceptionally good, plainly cooked seafood worthy of my native Boston. Parke's in Beauchamp Place was packed full of the flashiest members of society, and although the food tasted of little, the frou-frou presentation was spectacular – your bowl of soup would arrive garnished with all the floral arts of Moyses Stevens. The trattoria scene was lively too: Mario and Franco and their acolyte, Alvar, were (perhaps) the three trendiest head waiters on earth, and their respective establishments attracted London's mercanti (or glitterari).

But Londoners only began to talk about food with the arrival of Anton Mossiman at the Dorchester Hotel in the 1970s. He featured in the glossy magazines and became the first media celebrity chef. He abandoned nouvelle cuisine as soon as was decent, but food was firmly on the middle-class agenda. By the time I began to write about restaurants for *Harpers & Queen* in 1981, Langan's was the hot ticket in town, and Le Caprice was undergoing painful birth pangs. The first restaurant boom rose and fell with the fortunes of the Big Bang, the yuppies and the overheated property market of the late 1980s. The second, bigger boom seems to be less volatile: residents are dining out more often, more people invade London to eat, and London is called 'Restaurant capital of the world'. It certainly it is one of the small handful of world eating capitals, and for that we should say grace. Amen.

Introduction

Five centuries of city food

Cathy Ross

'And this Cookes Row is very necessary to the city: and according to Plato in Gorgius, next to physic, is the office of cooks as part of a city'.
John Stow, *The Survey of London*, 1598

In reminding his readers of the importance of cooks to city life, John Stow, writing in the 16th century, was paraphrasing William Fitzstephen, writing in the 12th century. Fitzstephen had also quoted Plato and identified the presence of public eating places as one of the distinguishing marks of London's civilisation. Today, 400 years after Stow, Plato's point remains. Although eating out in London at the end of the 20th century is vastly different in every superficial detail from eating out in Stow's day, it still remains 'very necessary to the city', the support system for every aspect of London's social, economic and cultural life.

This book, together with the accompanying exhibition, provides a broad map of eating out in London over the last five centuries. At this broad level the basic points of reference have to be the establishments through which Londoners ate outside their homes. But even a simple survey of these is no easy task: from victualling houses, Livery Company halls and taverns, through chop houses and Pleasure Gardens, gentleman's clubs, restaurants, and working men's cafés, bistros, sushi bars and gastropubs – the list of names under which these establishments have described themselves is immense. And although all have food in common, each is the product of particular circumstances and is not, therefore, necessarily related to any other.

The list of questions raised by this broad survey is equally immense. What were the processes of economic change at work in any one period? What does eating out in public tell us about other areas of social relations? This short introduction can only flag up three of the most basic questions, to sketch in outline the main themes that will be explored later in more detail.

First, who was eating out? From a 20th-century standpoint it is tempting to assume that every citizen of London, in whatever period, had some cause to eat out at some point in their lives. Whilst there is no doubt that the two fundamental reasons for eating out – necessity, because work or travel takes you away from home, and pleasure – are universal facts of life affecting the behaviour of all people at all times, it does not follow that eating out in the past was universally familiar. Until the late 19th century much of London's eating out was associated with male-dominated roles and activities: work, drinking, political discussion and public conviviality. One of the big

2. The Londoners' Meal Service, Millbank School Westminster, September 1940. The Service provided cooked meals for those without gas or electricity because of bomb damage during the Blitz.

shifts in eating out during the last 500 years is the full accommodation of women from the late 19th century onwards, mirroring the march of women into the work force and public life. Later in the 20th century children also began to be accommodated, as the novel idea that families could eat out together for fun began to take hold. Equally inconceivable to many Londoners in the past would have been the notion that eating out for pleasure rather than necessity was a legitimate activity on which to spend time and money. Again it is only really in the 0th century that eating out for pleasure has become part of everyday life for the majority and not just for the wealthy or comfortably-off minority.

Who made eating out possible? Who was either doing the cooking or paying the cook? Here the biggest sea-change is the transition from a medieval city culture, in which skilled trades such as cooking were controlled by guilds, to a modern market economy. By the end of the 17th century, and certainly by the 18th century, eating out in London was recognisably modern in that it was being driven both by market demand and by small entrepreneurs who saw in London golden opportunities for turning food into profit. As the opportunities for profit enlarged, alongside population increase and the spread of affluence, so the small entrepreneur was joined by catering companies, and 'the victualling trade' turned into 'the restaurant industry' with mammoth companies such as Jo Lyons & Co. Ltd supplying thousands of meals a day through their many outlets. Eating out over the last five centuries must stand as one of the most successful chapters in the history of modern British business, with a track record of nothing but increase in markets, profits, outlets and the scale of ambitions.

Thirdly, what did Londoners eat when they ate out? Here again the general dynamic is one of increase – an increasing choice of food and also increasing sophistication in the preparation and presentation of dishes. In 1500 the diet remained anchored to the medieval staples of bread, cheese and meat. Change came from the late 16th century as London's position at the centre of European trade affected the foods and culinary practices that found their way into the city's eating houses. New arrivals, such as chocolate and coffee, turtle soup and *boeuf à la mode*, penetrated even further into Londoners' eating habits with the trickle-down of food fashions to merchants and tradesmen from the nobility and gentry. Science and technology have also played their part in the increasing sophistication of Londoners' diets, notably through the invention of refrigeration.

Despite new arrivals, the status of meat, and roast beef in particular, remained high. Characterisations of the English as a meat-eating nation with a tendency to gluttony are thick on the ground from the 16th century, and, as we shall see, the English themselves subscribed to and took pride in this definition of nationhood. Inevitably the cult of meat is clearly visible on the map of London's eating-out establishments, from 16th-century cookshops and 18th-century chop houses to 20th-century grill rooms and steak houses. By the late 20th century, however, London's pride in its restaurants is no longer bound up with roast beef but with the astonishing variety of ethnic foods and cuisines found here, a variety said to be unrivalled by any other city on earth. The arrival of new cuisines, and cooking skills related to eating traditions other than English, has been a momentous and particularly enriching change in the recent story of eating out in London.

The increasing choice of food available in London has underlined social diversity as well as cultural diversity. Food, perhaps more than anything else can identify such amorphous concepts as taste, class and status: you are what you eat. Inevitably, London's eateries have reflected, and still do, the ebb and flow of more fundamental divisions within society, particularly those related to wealth. Ever-expanding choice is also bound up with changing social attitudes, particularly towards pleasure. As increasing numbers of Londoners, from the 17th century onwards, came to associate eating out with notions of comfort, civility, pleasure and amusement, so it became a virtue of city life, rather than a wretched necessity or an immoral luxury. Today's huge consumer choice is in part a testament to pleasure becoming respectable in British society.

The final point to be made by way of introduction is that eating out in London, whether for need or for pleasure, has been one of the most important ingredients in the city's cultural and creative energy over the past five centuries. There are many examples of eating out providing the arena for the exchange of ideas, social contact and mutual support – from the Drapers Company gathering for their lavish annual feast in the late 16th century, to the Vorticist painters meeting at La Tour Eiffel restaurant in the early 20th century. For William Fitzstephen in the 12th century the value of a public place providing ready-cooked food was mainly felt by travellers: 'however great the number of soldiers or strangers that enters or leaves the city at any hour of the day or night, they may turn in there if they please, and refresh themselves according to their inclination; so that the former have no occasion to fast too long or the latter to leave the city without dining'. The story of eating out in London over the last 500 years demonstrates that feeding travellers is just one benefit of many, and that the presence of professional cooks is indeed, as Plato identified, a fundamental prerequisite of a well-functioning city.

16th century

Hazel Forsyth

Throughout the 16th century, London exerted a gravitational pull on people, capital, goods and provisions. The phenomenal growth in population, from about 33,000 in 1500 to around a quarter of a million by the end of the century, provoked much concern, for soon, augured James I '... England will only be London...'.[1] Such rapid growth placed huge demands on the city's ability to support and feed its inhabitants, and in 1516 ten bread ovens were specially built on London Bridge for 'the best advantage for reliefe of the poore citizens, when the need should require'.[2] Although average prices multiplied by a factor of five between 1530 and 1640, there were peaks and troughs in the rate of inflation, and food prices fluctuated considerably. During the 16th century, dairy products and some meats (especially mutton) were fairly expensive, prices remaining high because the demand for these foods continued to exceed the supplies available.[3] Places to eat outside the home were essential to the well-being of the populace but also provided an important social function in the urban community. Until well into the 17th century rich and poor lived in close proximity, cheek by jowl in the City centre, and this social mingling was reflected in the mixture of low- and high-class eating-out establishments catering for all tastes and pockets.

What were the eating-out habits of Londoners during the 16th century? Where did they eat and with whom? What did they eat and when? Such deceptively simple questions are extremely difficult to answer, for while there are plenty of documents relating to the supply of food and domestic upper-class dining during this period, there is far less information about the types of food and drink consumed outside of the home. Much of the evidence concerns only a small sector of society; and information on the diet and eating habits of the poor and lower classes is mostly lacking.[4] To compound the problem, pictorial sources are virtually non-existent, and literary and documentary sources only begin to provide a comprehensive picture for eating out in the capital from the mid-17th century. For all the richness of Elizabethan poetry and drama, there are few allusions to eating-out establishments. We know little about the food consumed in inns during this period, and until the beginning of the next century taverns offered little more than a piece of bread with a pint of wine. We do know however, that the basic structure of London's catering trade remained the same until at least the 18th century, although outlets adapted to match changing

3. Detail from Frans Franken II (1581–1642). *Lazarus at the Rich Man's Table*, 1605.

fashions and social expectations. Hot nourishing meals and ready-to-eat foods were provided by inns, ale-houses and cookshops the forerunners of modern hotels, restaurants, pubs and snack bars, and for many Londoners the Livery Company hall was an important venue for convivial dining and corporate entertaining.

COOKSHOPS – TUDOR FAST FOOD

In his *Description of London* published in 1174, the chronicler William Fitzstephen provides a graphic account of a *publica coquina* (public eating-house or cookshop), open day and night, at which 'every day, according to the season, may be found viands of all kinds, roast, fried, and boiled, fish large and small, coarser meat for the poor and more delicate for the rich such as venison, fowls, and small birds... [t]his indeed is the public cookery, and very convenient to the city, and a distinguishing mark of civilisation.'[5] Strategically sited on a prime spot adjacent to the Vintry wine wharves and the principal docks of the City, this cookshop attracted merchants, watermen, travellers and 'rich knights'. Probably then, and certainly by the mid-13th century, there were several cookshops in the vicinity. Four hundred years later John Stow, in his *Survey of London*, referred to a 'Cookes Row' in the Vintry[6] and identified two further catering communities in the commercial heart of the City, in Eastcheap and Bread Street. Cookshops were also to be found by Westminster Gate, offering ale, wine, bread and fat ribs of beef, and in the area around Smithfield.[7]

The demand for these establishments was obviously considerable, for Stow relates: 'such as were disposed to be merry, met not to dine and sup in taverns (for they dressed not meats to be sold) but to the Cooks [cookshop], where they called for meat what they liked'.[8] Surprising though it may seem today, documentary and archaeological evidence suggests that very few Londoners had an oven or kitchen and even those with access to a hearth mostly lacked the elaborate equipment needed for roasting and basting. Cookshops, therefore, played a crucial role in the diet of Londoners, offering quickly prepared hot meals for those without cooking facilities or the time and inclination to prepare meals for themselves. Although we do not know how many cookshops there were in London during the 16th century, it is likely that the demand for cheap ready-to-eat foods increased after the Reformation and subsequent Dissolution of the Monasteries. Until the Dissolution (1536–39) the religious orders were primarily responsible for the care of the poor, and daily doles of leftover food were distributed at monastery gates. Thereafter, paupers were increasingly reliant upon donations from wealthy citizens and municipal charity. Whilst historians question the degree to which the poor were affected by the loss of monastic charity, London was the first city to introduce a system of compulsory subscriptions for poor relief, and evidence suggests that increasing amounts of money were distributed to paupers by the end of the century. This new-found purchasing power must have enabled many of them to buy their own food directly from cookshops and ale-houses, thereby stimulating trade and contributing to the demand for cheap places to eat out. Even though we know very little about the food and

clients of cookshops during the 16th century, pictorial and cartographic evidence provides some information about the structure and internal layout of these premises. Joris Hoefnagel's painting entitled *A Fête at Bermondsey*, c.1570, depicting cookshop catering on a commercial scale, is the only image of a functional cookshop for this early period of London's history.[9] Inside, joints sizzle over the roasting range as fat drips into pans below, shelves support partly prepared dishes and utensils, while pies and meats are served up on pewter plates. The second source of evidence comes from Ralph Treswell's pictorial surveys of the cookshops in Giltspur Street and Cock Lane, Smithfield, of 1611 (Fig. 5). The ground plans show the extent of the buildings and the vast commercial ovens and ranges within them.[10]

From the medieval period onwards, cooks and cookshops tend to receive a bad press. In order to practise their trade within the City and suburbs all cooks had to be members of the Cooks' Company, and the Master and Wardens had direct supervision over all practitioners, exacting severe penalties for any misdemeanour. All victuallers were required by law to provide good and wholesome food, but the frequent imposition of regulatory measures suggests that high standards were difficult to enforce and malpractice was not uncommon.[11] The distasteful image of the cook with

4. Detail from Joris Hoefnagel's *A Fête at Bermondsey* (c.1570) showing cookshop catering for a wedding feast. The cook supervises the roasted meats, and food is passed to the waiters from a serving hatch.

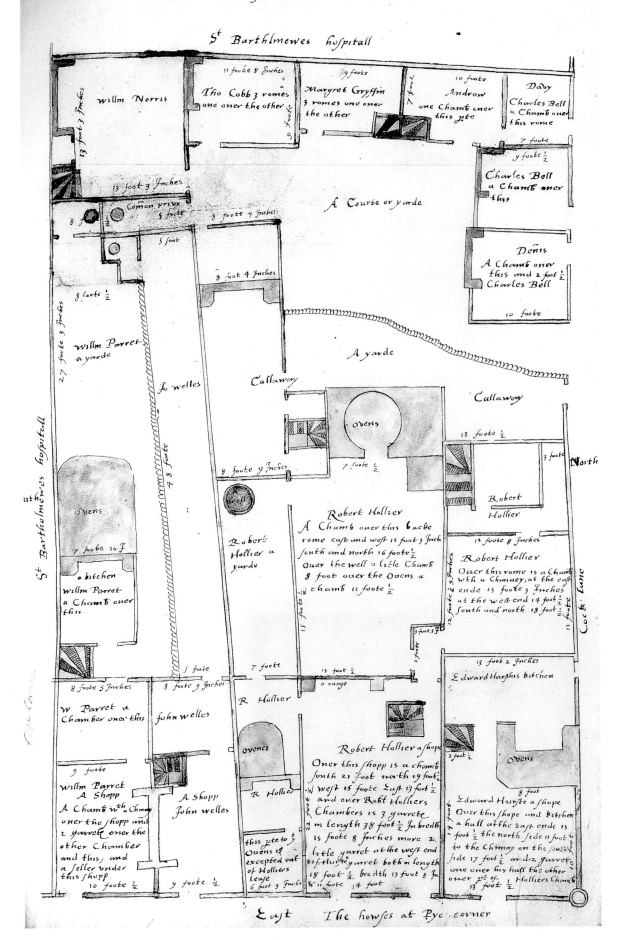

his suppurating syphilitic sore is encapsulated by Chaucer in his character sketch of
Hodge of Ware, Cook of London. Hodge was pilloried by the proprietor of the Tabard
Inn in Southwark for his reheated pies, parsimonious application of sauces,
unappetising pasties, wilting parsley garnishes and fly-ridden shop.[12] Even if one
allows for a certain amount of occupational rivalry, the character and professional
abilities of Hodge must have rung some familiar bells with Chaucer's contemporaries!
Documents and literature for the 14th and 15th centuries indicate that only the lower
classes and poor frequented cookshops in London[13] and there is no reason to suppose
that habits changed during the 16th century, although precise evidence is lacking.

Cookshop food was supplemented by hot and cold snacks available from street
hawkers, who plied their wares throughout the metropolis at specific times of day.
These served poor and affluent alike, the former grabbing a quick bite on the hoof,
the latter purchasing cakes and buns to eat in more salubrious surroundings. Whilst
shopkeepers railed against this itinerant trade, the hawkers of ready-to-eat foods were
indispensable to Londoners, and because they were popular like the cookshops they
continued to flourish.

THE ALE-HOUSE – 'Would I were in an alehouse in London!'[14]

The food provided by a standard cookshop was little different from that offered in a
typical ale-house, and occasionally cookshops and ale-houses combined.[15] As the
name implies, the primary function of the ale-house was to sell ale, an infusion of
malt; but from the mid-16th century the more potent beer, a mixture of malt and
hops, became increasingly popular, 'to the detryment of many Englysshe men …
[since] it doth make a man fatte, and doth inflate the belly…'.[16]

Ale-houses tended to attract idle, lewd, young 'luskish' clients, including the
criminal fraternity, and attempts to curb the excesses of drinking and 'great disorders
daylie used' therein met with limited success. Although the authorities tried to restrict
the numbers of tippling houses and impose regulatory control, the number of
unlicensed premises proliferated.[17] By 1613 there were over 1,000 licensed ale-houses
in the City alone, and some of these had between 200–300 barrels in the cellar.[18]
Most stocked a variety of beers and ales including beer 'prepared in bottles with
spices, an exquisite drink, but very strong which froths' and the 'common beer drunk
among the least well-off' called 'small beer'. Some specialised in a particular brew
such as Lambeth ale, china-ale and mum (a kind of stout with roasted malt).[19] Cock-
ale, a speciality of the ale-house/brothel, believed to promote fecundity, was a
revolting concoction of raisins, dates, nutmeg and a freshly killed cockerel steeped in
a cask of beer. Tasting a glass of cock-ale in 1698, Ned Ward 'could not conceive it to
be anything but a mixture of small beer and treacle'. He was alluding to the ale-house
proprietors' trick of mixing ale with resin (treacle) and salt, the former to reduce the
capacity of the drinking vessel so that the unwitting customer received a short
measure, whilst the salt increased their thirst![20] Ale-houses provided very basic cheap
food to accompany their alcoholic beverages; snacks such as spiced buns and cake

5. The substantial ovens and
ranges in the cookshops of
Cock Lane and Giltspur Street
can be seen on Treswell's
survey of properties in Smithfield
during the early 17th century.

steeped in ale, as well as bread and cheese. Roasted meats began to be served at midday and occasionally more exotic fare was eaten, but this was usually brought in by the customer.[21] Most of the London ale-houses were little more than a single room, but some were large enough to offer bed and board and facilities for regular gatherings of clubs and societies. No tipling was allowed after nine o'clock at night, and ale-houses were shut on Sunday. Gambling was forbidden, and no drink could be served from a silver vessel.[22] Women could visit ale-houses on their own, although only the lower classes would have done so without an escort.[23]

LIVERY COMPANY FEASTS – CORPORATE ENTERTAINING

An altogether different form of public eating was the Livery Company dinner, and this 16th-century form of corporate entertaining provides the best evidence for eating out in the period. Livery Companies developed from the religious and craft guilds of medieval London, the term 'livery' referring to the suit of clothing allocated to members annually. Each company had responsibility for the regulation of a particular trade, appointing officials to inspect the wares produced and sold. Official premises or halls were used for inspection, arbitration and charitable relief and no one could practice a trade within the City of London unless they belonged to a company which gave them the 'freedom' to do so.

The dinners were a combination of magnificence and beneficence, and meals were provided by the City Companies for members at specific times in the year, the most important coinciding with the feast day of the company's patron saint and the election and appointment of a new Master. Dinners were held to reinforce social bonds and helped to promote business between companies, affluent individuals and the highest strata of society. For the election, three dinners were provided on three consecutive days. Comparatively modest meals of roasted mutton, goose and capon (castrated chicken) with codlings (stewed apples in a rosewater and sugar syrup), spiced biscuits, cakes, buns and comfits were consumed on the first two days, designed to sustain, but not to spoil the appetite for the great feast itself. On the third day, after a church service, the whole livery assembled at the hall for the Election Dinner, which usually took place at one o'clock or shortly thereafter. Those unable to attend through infirmity were not forgotten.[24] Nor were the poor. Liverymen were allocated their portion of the feast in carefully calculated amounts according to their status within the company, while the poor tended to receive gifts of roasted beef and venison pasties the following day.[25] Remnants from the feast and kitchen leftovers were also distributed to paupers who loitered by the hall gates and doors. Sometimes the companies' social conscience meant that the traditional great feast was reduced, so that part of the allowance could be devoted to the relief of the poor, and in times of national dearth or plague years many companies went without a dinner, the Drapers doing so for several years in succession.[26]

The total cost of the dinners varied considerably but averaged between £20 and £80 per feast throughout the 16th century, substantial sums, when the daily wage of a

kitchen skivvy was eight pence.[27] The meals consumed convey information about the kinds of foods purchased and the costs incurred, but these feasts were lavish expressions of hospitality and it is possible that discounts were offered for bulk orders.[28] If the Master was also the Lord Mayor, largess was extended to senior members of other companies, and often to visiting dignitaries and distinguished guests, and on these occasions expenses usually exceeded £100.[29]

Livery Company archives contain much evidence for the management and provision of feasts during the 16th century, with important information about the types of food available, the quantities consumed and the meals and tastes of the period. Especially valuable is the unique manuscript 'Dinner Book' of the Drapers' Company, which provides comprehensive evidence for dining from 1564 to 1602.[30] For the most part, the menus relate to the top three tables in the Hall, to the table in the room behind for the Wardens and other officers, and to the Ladies' table in the parlour. The top table was reserved for the Court, the side tables for guests and their wives and the senior livery. Significantly the guests' table was adjacent to the cupboard or buffet, resplendent with silver and silver-gilt plate – a dazzling and ostentatious display of wealth and status.

Unfortunately we do not know how many people attended the feasts, but during the course of the 16th century thousands of Londoners must have dined in Livery Company halls. As a result, we cannot calculate the precise food allocation for each

Above left
6. Presented to the Mercers' Company by William Burde, and made in Germany in 1554, this silver-gilt and enamel clockwork wagon travels across the table. The tun, or barrel, dispensed rosewater over the hands of diners.

Above right
7. A 16th-century receptacle for salt with a protective cover. During a feast the Great Salt was placed opposite the host at the top of the table; to sit near it was a mark of distinction. Lesser salts were used on the side tables.

table, although numbers are sometimes given for the top tables and suppliers' accounts shed some light. In 1566, for example, Mr Lucas the Pikemonger, supplied the Drapers' with thirty-six pike purchased by the inch; six at 24 in, twelve at 20 in and twelve at 18 in. Of these, seventeen and perhaps the largest at 24 in[31] were consumed by the top tables, leaving the remainder to be divided amongst the rest of the livery, perhaps 140 people.[32]

The range of foods consumed by the companies was extensive. Between 1564 and 1602 the Drapers' accounts and dinner books include 139 different products. Some foods occur in every feast, such as the large and beautifully decorated marchepanes (a baked confection of almonds, rosewater, sugar, eggs and wafers), often as large as a tray and garnished with a 'subteltie' or device alluding to the company (made from coloured sugar and wax), surrounded by biscuits, caraway seeds and comfits (sugar-coated spices). Pellet-shaped comfits, the 16th-century equivalent of the modern indigestion tablet, were enjoyed as sweets, but were equally favoured for their digestive benefits and were generally consumed at the end of the meal in the dessert or 'banquet'.[33] The Livery Companies seem to have bought their comfits direct from the confectioner and may well have stipulated particular coatings and colourings to suit the occasion. Equally ubiquitous was the supply of cakes, buns and spice bread and the decorative wafers which accompanied the spiced wine 'hypocras'.[34]

Left
8. *This Large Food Display* by Georg Flegel (1566–1638) depicts part of a stepped buffet laden with precious objects, sweetmeats and confectionery for the banquet or dessert course. Wooden trenchers are stacked on top of a cheese, and the box in the foreground contains candied fruit.

Above
9. Many kinds of festive food are represented in this beautifully rendered *Kitchen Scene* by Adriaen van Nieulandt (1616).

Much of the menu was meat based: pork, brawn, beef, lamb, chicken, rabbit, venison, goose, duck (mallard and teal), woodcock, greenplover (lapwing), lark, snipe, pigeon, quail, swan, heron, crane, partridge and the newly introduced turkey.[35] On exceptional occasions, such as the Merchant Taylors' feast for James I,[36] pheasant, peacock, ruff (a type of wader), doves, godwits, martins, teal and even owls and cuckoos were consumed. To foreigners, the range and quantity of meat consumed by the English was astonishing: in London, as Italian merchant Alessandro Magno remarked, '... it is almost impossible to believe that they could eat so much meat in one City alone'.[37] But even English commentators found some of their countrymen's appetites remarkable, and the 'delicat meate' and exotic fare provided by Livery Companies were regarded as being equal in range and quality to that of the nobility, for they would 'seldome regard anie thing that the butcher usuallie killeth, but reject the same as not worthie...'.[38] The only limitations on the choice of meats were the periodic availability of the migratory bird species and an occasional complaint from Court concerning the consumption of venison, which was greatly prized as a high-status food. To ensure adequate provision some of the less abundant and migratory bird species were acquired in advance, and the Drapers' accounts record payments for food to fatten up quails and cygnets for the table.[39]

Fish was the second most important feast food unless the dinner took place on a Fish Day or during Lent when the meals were devoid of meat.[40] Sturgeon and pike were the mainstays, but the Thames was also full of 'fat and sweet salmons' and eels[41] for roasting and baking.[42] Lampreys, smelt, cod, ling, dace, crab, oysters, tench, mullet, sole, bream, plaice, whiting, roach, haddock, flounders, shrimps and turbot were all eaten at feast dinners.[43] Britts (young herrings or sprats) were consumed in quantity, an interesting precursor to the formal whitebait dinners of the 18th and 19th centuries. The accounts make a clear distinction between 'green', 'fresh', and 'olde', or preserved fish, the latter usually powdered or salted.[44] Carp occurs in the Drapers' accounts from 1567, and '... seemeth to be scant, sith it is not long since that kind of fish was brought over into England'.[45] Marine mammals were also regarded as 'fish' and on one occasion 'fresh sele' (seal) was eaten by the Grocers, who seem to have enjoyed a wider range of fish than many other companies in the period.[46] Evidence for the consumption of whales is rare, and although dolphin and porpoise bones have been recovered from medieval and post-medieval domestic deposits in London, cetacean flesh was not consumed by the Livery Companies during the 16th century.[47]

During the century a wide range of 'green meates' was available, and street hawkers sold artichokes, white-heart and savoy cabbages, onions, turnips, broccoli, radishes, peas, beans, carrots, cauliflowers and asparagus.[48] It was not until the latter part of the century, however, that vegetables began to be widely eaten for, according to William Harrison in 1577, 'the poor and gentry alike are beginning to use melons, radishes, turnips, gourds, cucumbers, parsneps, carrots, cabbages and all kinds of salad herbs'.[49] Even so, hardly any vegetables or salad stuffs were eaten by the Livery Companies, for reasons which are not entirely clear. Potage (a strong broth with chopped herbs,

Above
10. *The Vegetable Seller* by Joachim Beuckelaer (*c*.1530–73). The sheer abundance of fruit and vegetables serves to emphasise improved techniques in husbandry and the cultivation of new varieties.

Left
11. This detail from David Tenier the Younger's (1644) *Kitchen Scene* shows luxury 'display' foods. After roasting, swans were sewn back into their skins, set on pastry 'coffins' and decorated.

12. These beechwood roundels are decorated on one side only; the plain surface may have been used for sticky sweetmeats during the banquet course.

vegetables, oatmeal, salt and sometimes stewed meat) was a major component of the everyday diet for the lower classes in particular, and vegetables may have been excluded from the feast menu because they were not special enough.[50] But perhaps the Livery Companies preferred traditional, high-protein foods and wished simply to abide by customary practice.

Fruit, however, was consumed by all the companies throughout the 16th century and served according to the season.[51] There is no reference to the newly introduced apricot, but plums and prunes, raisins, currants, quince, gooseberries, mulberries, barberries, figs and apples were cooked in tarts, boiled and made into puree and sauces.[52] The high-pectin fruits were converted into glittering jewel-like marmalades, flat discs of fruit syrups decorated with elaborate geometric patterns and comfits.[53] Citrus fruits were transformed into succades, candied sweetmeats, and the juices were used for sauces and flavourings. Fresh fruits, particularly apples and pears and occasionally grapes,[54] were eaten as appetisers or for dessert,[55] and by the late 16th century Londoners could be seen 'munching them in the streets and at places of public amusement all day long'.[56] In the Livery Hall, strawberries and cherries make a rare appearance,[57] but both were readily available on the street from at least the mid-15th century, and cherries threaded on short sticks, were sold by hawkers crying 'Ripe, Cherry, Ripe!'.[58] An amusing, perhaps aprocryphal, account is provided by Father

Busino in the early 17th century. He claims it was the fashion for City belles and their admirers to visit the orchards around the metropolis and there gorge themselves, sometimes competing to see who could eat the most at one sitting. At one such gathering a young woman devoured an astonishing 20lbs of cherries, beating her rival by a mere 2lbs. It seems that she suffered a severe illness shortly thereafter.[59]

Hardly any cheese[60] and not much milk was bought by the Livery Companies, but vast quantities of cream, butter and eggs were eaten. The absence of fine cheese from the Livery feast menu is a little surprising, because English cheeses with translucent rinds and distinctive stamped designs of figures, letters, flowers and animals were greatly appreciated on the Continent for their beauty and quality.[61] But perhaps because cheese was commonly eaten in the ale-house with bread and beer it was not considered sufficiently luxurious for a feast.[62]

In addition to spice breads, the bakers supplied fresh white, and 'cheat' wheaten (grey/yellow wheat coloured) manchets (rolls) and loaves, as well as stale white bread which was presumably used to thicken sauces and give substance to puddings.[63] Some of the stale loaves were used for trenchers, slices with the crusts pared off to form square, inch-thick 'plates'. Small two- by three-inch strips of stale bread were also used for individual helpings of salt. The older the bread the better, and trencher bread which was four days old was deemed 'convenyent and agreable'.[64] By the mid-century wooden trenchers were beginning to replace those made of bread and for a while the Livery Companies used both. In 1566 the Drapers paid 10s for 276 wooden trenchers, but this change brought increased work for the poor kitchen maids, who often spent two days scraping them clean after the feasts.[65] Bread trenchers, stale or fresh, were passed to the destitute at the kitchen doors.

Treswell's Surveys show that even the richest Livery Companies had fairly small halls and mass catering must have proved a logistical nightmare.[66] Some indication of how the halls may have looked during an Election Dinner is provided by Samuel Pepys, who attended the Lord Mayor's Banquet in 1663.[67] Under each salt was a Bill of Fare, with a seating list at the end of each table. Pepys was disgruntled to find that no change of napkins or trenchers were provided and guests had to drink from earthen pitchers and wooden bowls.[68] Throughout the 16th century, meals were served by stewards and also by the young Batchelors of the company who had to wait till everyone else was served before partaking themselves. Sometimes this caused murmuring 'and mislike that they were kept soe longe', and in 1588 the Batchelors of the Drapers' 'contemptuouslie departed' without their dinners 'using some harde speech and apparent shewes of their discontent'.[69]

COOKS — 'We Cooks of London, which work early and late'.[70]

What effect did the cooks have on the eating-out habits of Londoners in this period? Many of those employed by the Livery Companies and the proprietors of inns ran the equivalent of a modern catering company, providing feast and party foods as and when required. Stephen Trigell, the Drapers' cook, received numerous payments from the Company for food cooked at home, including baked venison and venison pasties, chicken pies, marchepanes, custards and tarts.[71] For 'dressing the dinners' for three days, Trigell was paid 40 shillings, and he recieved additional payments for supplies and pre-prepared food.

A good cook, wrote Thomas Cogan, 'is a good jewell ... to be much made of'. But, cautions Russell writing in the late 15th century, they should not assume airs beyond their station and must obey the Usher/Marshall whether they like it or not.[72] Russell urged his readers to treat cooks with care, since with 'theire newe conceytes, choppynge, stampynge and gryndynge' they continually invent tempting new dishes which 'provoke the... peple to perelles of passage' endangering their lives.[73] By the mid-century, however, culinary experimentation was esteemed, and he 'is counted the finest Cooke nowadays, than can invent new fashions, new divices and new disguises'.[74]

But while culinary skill was generally admired, social commentators were quick to emphasise that the plain, wholesome tradition of English cooking was being eroded and subverted by foreign and particularly Flemish practice. Fashionable dishes were small and extraordinarily fussy.[75] From the 1570s, blame shifted to French cooks and French cuisine: and for the 'number of dishes and change of meat, the nobilitie of England (whose Cookes are for the most part musicall-headed Frenchmen and strangers) doo most exceed...'.[76] Although French cuisine was popular in domestic upper-class dining, French eating-houses did not become a feature of London catering until well into the next century.

London has always been subject to foreign culinary influence, but the extent to which continental food affected eating-out establishments during the century is difficult to assess. After all, the best cooking is always a blend of tradition and innovation. As arbiters of taste, the Citizen Cooks of London had a fair degree of autonomy and the more enterprising and resourceful among them must have been keen to experiment with exciting new ingredients, recipes and styles of presentation, in turn influencing the palates and culinary choices of their patrons. Nonetheless, foreign travel writers all point to distinct differences between English and continental food tradition, suggesting that, amongst the 'middling sort of people' at least, plain English fare with its heavy emphasis on roasted meats was preferred. For some, this was a matter of cultural pride, a culinary xenophobia that reached its apotheosis in the 18th century.

While the most prestigious, high-profile catering positions were occupied by men, there were many women cooks in London. Skills varied considerably and inn and tavern proprietors obtained the services of individuals who specialised in a particular branch of the catering industry, as well as providing reliable, good-quality and cost-effective service. Some acquired such expertise that nicknames were given; thus Goodwife Odye, a victualler in Tower Street, was generally known as 'wife mampuddinge'.[77]

13. *A Cook with Food*
(*c.*1630–40) by Frans Snyders. The calm quality of this image belies the frenetic activity that usually accompanies food preparation.

Focus

Street Food – Gingerbread, Sugar-loaves and Mechanical Vending Machines Hazel Forsyth

■

■

■

■

Alongside the foods provided by the main catering establishments, Londoners could also obtain sustenance from transient retailers and entrepreneurs. Hawkers offered shellfish, nuts, fresh fruit and cheap hot snacks such as baked apples, pancakes, dumplings, boiled sheep's feet, eel pies, peas in the pod, muffins, rolls, oat cakes and spiced gingerbread.[78] In theatres, apples, pears and nuts were sold in season, and pippins, a newly introduced variety of apple, were given by youths to their sweethearts.[79]

Above left

14. and 15. These images of street sellers come from Marcellus Lauron's *Cries of London* series (*c.*1687) engraved by Pierce Tempest. Hot Bak'd Wardens, or stewed pears, were especially popular in winter. Colly Molly Puffe, a familiar sight in the latter part of the 17th century, derived his name from his cry advertising gingerbread, fruit and meat pies, cakes and puff pastries.

Certain localities specialised in particular types of food: Islington, Hackney, Holloway and Deptford were noted for their cheesecakes, and the Lodge in Hyde Park sold syllabubs, cheesecake and fresh cow's milk.[80] Hot puddings, pies, nuts, oranges and gingerbread could be bought from stalls on Fleet Bridge; pancakes were a speciality of Rosemary Lane; and pies were sold at The Farthing Pie House in Marylebone Fields.[81]

Food was a popular ingredient of fairs and festivals. Hearths to prepare roasted oxen and toasted bread were set up on the ice during the Frost Fairs, while booths became taverns, ale-houses and cookshops selling plum cakes, gingerbread, hot pudding pies, boiled mutton, bread and cheese and a variety of alcoholic and non-alcoholic hot drinks. The demand for fast food at fairs was such that Smithfield properties were leased annually to provide extra catering facilities for the great fair of St Bartholomew.[82] At major celebrations and ceremonial events, the City conduits ran with red and white wine and occasionally food was provided for the onlookers. At one memorable

Lord Mayor's Show, the Grocers' provided 36lbs of nutmegs, 114lbs of ginger, 24lbs dates and 50 sugar-loaves, which 'were thrown about the streetes from those which sate on the griffyns and camells'.[83]

By the end of the 17th century, an increasing number of victualling establishments provided entertainment alongside food, usually with live performers, acrobats, jugglers, musicians and singers. But the enterprising proprietor of the Black Horse in Hosier Lane offered a 'new Mathematical Fountain', a glass contraption 9ft high and 12ft long 'in which is a tavern, a coffee house and a brandy shop', each section dispensing hot and cold drinks (sack, white wine, claret, coffee, tea, plain, cherry and raspberry brandy, geneva, usquebaugh and punch). Charles Butcher offered this delight for 6d a view and 2d per glass.[84] His ingenious mechanism was derived from Henry van Etten's early 17th-century 'magick barrel' and Henry Winstanley's Water-Theatre in Hyde Park.[85]

Winstanley's Water-Theatre opened in 1703 and operated at four o'clock on Monday afternoons. Above the concealed vat supporting a large tea and coffee pot fastened by ropes, were trays from which the drinks could be dispensed to the people of highest rank. After Winstanley's death his widow continued the performance with numerous modifications, so that by 1712 six types of wine were on offer. The best brandy and biscuits were given to those in the boxes and pit, with geneva, cherry beer and cider to the first gallery. A year later, the 'curious barrel' was converted to a 'Spring Garden' dispensing, mineral waters, milk, ale, beer, syllabubs, cake, biscuits and cheese cake.[86]

17th century

The period between 1600–1700 saw a rapid increase in the population of London, and an expansion of catering provision. Inns, taverns, ale-houses and cookshops proliferated and flourished because society demanded them, and that demand led to increasing specialisation, innovation and commercialisation. From the first decades of the 17th century taverns and ale-houses began to provide a wider range of food, and the fixed-price meal was introduced. By the end of the century cooks no longer monopolised the cookshop trade, and hot meals were supplied by anyone with entrepreneurial initiative.

The advent of the 'London season' in the early years of the century brought new eating-out establishments and gastronomic experiences.[1] More Londoners could afford to eat out for pleasure, and specialised outlets opened to cater for this demand. A luxury eating-house opened at Shaver's Hall in Piccadilly; some of the Bagnios and Hummums provided coffee-drinking facilities, and dining rooms appeared in Pleasure Gardens. French cuisine became increasingly popular amongst the middle and upper classes, and new French eating-houses offered ragout (highly seasoned stewed meat and vegetables), morells, frogs, snails, sauces and new salads.[2] Coffee- and chocolate-houses also opened to supply new, hot non-alcoholic beverages.

Dinner remained the main meal of the day, but mealtimes began to change during the 17th century, reflecting the social status of diners for the first time: '[t]he English eat a great deal at Dinner, they rest a while, and to it again, till they have quite stuff'd their Paunch. Their Supper is moderate: Gluttons at noon, and abstinent at Night'.[3] Artisans, businessmen and the lower classes continued to eat at midday, but from about 1660 the middle classes started their main meal a little later, from one o'clock and sometimes at two o'clock. The upper classes and those with fashionable pretensions dined even later: 'why does any Body Dine before Four a clock in London?'.[4]

Although meat consumption remained high, vegetables were increasingly served, and a wider range of salads and fresh fruits were offered by hucksters, taverns, 'ordinaries' (offering fixed-price meals) and cookshops. By the end of the century roasted or boiled meats were increasingly accompanied by '5 or 6 Heaps of Cabbage, Carot, Turnips or some other Herbs or Roots, well pepper'd and salted and swimming in Butter'.[5]

19. A tiled sign from the Cock and Bottle Tavern, Cannon Street, early 18th century.

INNS, TAVERNS AND 'ORDINARIES'

'A tavern is an Academy of Debauchery…a Tipling School a degree above an Ale-house, where you may be drunk with more Credit…'. So wrote an anonymous pamphlet writer in 1675. To show that you are going to a 'tryal for your life', he continued, you must first appear at the Bar, where the Barmaid, bedecked with gaudy trinkets, sits 'like the Mother of Bacchus under her all-commanding Canopy'. Next comes the tavern-keeper, wearing a blue apron over his vast belly, who 'you would take for a Hogshead set on two stumps, mov'd by screws or clockwork'. His nose blazes like a comet and he 'infallibly pretends drought'. Thus, the writer suggests, a guest pays twice over for his drink, 'first to the Drawer and then to the Master'. Moreover, the guest is beguiled by the enticing food on offer, but must pay four times over for the privilege: first, for the meat, secondly for the dressing, thirdly for the sauce and fourthly for the fancy name; so that 'when they provide you with a Dinner you were better [to] keep open house all Christmas'.[6]

What were the inns, taverns and ordinaries of London really like in this period? William Harrison, writing in 1572, suggests that London inns were the worst in England, although he mitigates this statement with the comment that 'manie are there far better than the best I have heard of in anie forren countries'. The Italian Alessandro Magno was certainly impressed with the London Inn called Della Balla (The Ball), which offered a choice of two or three roast meats, or meat pies and savouries as an alternative, with fruit tarts, cheese and excellent wine.[7]

Harrison argued that tavern- and inn-keepers vied with each other to provide commodious and clean accommodation, quality and variety of wines, and good food and entertainment.[8] Vast sums were expended on the 'gorgeousness' of the signs at their doors 'wherein some doo consume thirtie or fortie pounds', an expenditure

Above
20.a,b,c. A selection of 17th-century tavern signs. The Ape and Apple from Philip Lane, The Leather Bottle from Leather Lane, Holborn and the Boar's Head from Eastcheap.

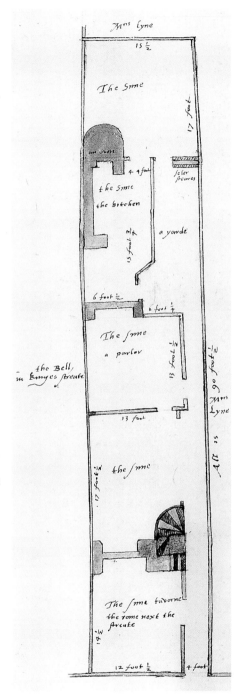

which most regarded as wholly worthwhile to advertise their business and emphasise their wealth and status.[9]

London taverns were located along the principal thoroughfares with particular concentrations near Whitehall and in the commercial and mercantile areas of the City. As Zetzner wrote in 1700: 'when the Stock Exchange has closed, it is into these premises that the traders pour; it is there that they discuss and finalise the biggest deals. Every merchant of any importance has for the morning and afternoon, his particular tavern where he may be found at certain hours. There are, all round the … Exchange, these establishments whose proprietors are themselves worth more than £50,000 sterling but who nevertheless serve their regular clients with their own hands, cap under arm'.[10]

In contrast, the inns were mostly located around the periphery of the metropolis, with clusters on the major axial routes out of the city, catering for travellers and carriers.[11] The carriers seem to have had favourite inns and taverns, as the list compiled with 'tedious toyle' by John Taylor in 1637 indicates. Every Friday night, for example, the carriers from St Albans lodged at the Peacocke in Aldersgate Street, while those from Aylesbury stayed at the George near Holborn Bridge, the Swan in the Strand, the Angel behind St Clement's Church and the Bell in Holborn.[12]

For a wide cross-section of Londoners, taverns were the focus of social life, providing food and drink in convivial and often very comfortable surroundings. The premises varied in size from single rooms often in a cellar or above a shop,[13] to multiple-roomed dwellings of twenty to

Far right
21. Thomas Larkine was the proprietor of Sun Tavern in King Street, Westminster when this survey was undertaken in 1611. By 1664 the tavern had 22 rooms. Samuel Pepys visited the Sun on several occasions.

22. This stoneware bottle from Frechen, Germany bears the personalised monogram of Pieter van den Ancker, a Dutchman who traded in French wines in London from 1654.

thirty hearths, occupying a substantial plot with a yard, outhouses, gardens and bowling greens.[14] Inventories of London taverns and inns in the period show that most had a series of named rooms for hire; often as many as eighteen in the larger establishments.[15] The names assigned to the rooms were used as a means of identification and sometimes described their function. Typical examples include the Common Heir Roome, a commodious space with simple, sparse furnishing for general use; the Oyster Roome (presumably for oyster suppers); the Organ and Musick Rooms; and the Darke Roome (which may have lacked windows or good light). More often, the names fall into the following categories: animals – Lion, Swan, Hare, Hart, Greyhound, Dove, Pye, Falcon, Nag's head; plant – Rose, Pomegranate; heraldic – Crown, Feathers, Mitre, King's Head, Queen's Head, King's Arms, Queen's Arms, Anchor and Dragon; astrological – Star, Sun, Moon, Half-Moon. Each room must have been decorated with a distinctive painted sign.

The principal rooms of the inn and tavern were the Bar, Tap Room, Drinking Rooms, Cellar and Kitchen. Patrons usually stepped directly from the entrance into the Bar, furnished with tables, benches, stools, a cistern, fireplace and in larger premises with a napkin press, spice cupboard and candle chest. Bells hung from a rack, one for each of the private rooms, and glass lanterns were placed for easy access.[16]

The furnishings in these rooms varied considerably, although most had a hearth and window. Valuations range from as little as £1 to over £14, and the quality of the room was probably reflected in the hire charge. The best rooms provided every comfort, with hangings, turkey-work upholstery, paintings, a looking glass, clock and often a closet or privy. Rooms were either booked in advance or requested on arrival. The fellows of the Royal Society made regular use of a private room in the Crown in Leadenhall Street for suppers and on 20 January 1666 for a meeting. Seven years later, the Society was presented with a bill from Mr Brandon, vintner, for expenses incurred in entertaining newly introduced Gresham College members. The total amount, £2 17s 9d, included payment for 18 quarts of wine (canary, rhenish and claret), small marchepanes, refined sugar, hire of plate, glasses, damask napkins, candles, pipes, replacement of a missing quart bottle and cleaning the room afterwards![17] The Livery Companies also used the facilities of a tavern for refreshment after a Search [a process

of quality control] and Ward Officers, responsible for the administration of City wards likewise invariably finished off their evening labours with a substantial supper in a nearby tavern.[18]

For businessmen 'a private room is made available where business is transacted over a glass of wine, and no one is disturbed until the bell is rung'.[19] Pepys was often invited to a tavern dinner by his business associates; the wining and dining literally employed to influence or curry favour. Thus although on one occasion Pepys recorded an enjoyable 'two or three dishes of meat well done', he was all too aware of his hosts' 'great designe…to get me concerned in a business of theirs…'.[20] At other times the tavern meals were genuine expressions of thanks for kindnesses or work done, and Pepys happily wrote of a midday fish dinner at the Dolphin, provided by two tar-merchants, 'and very merry we were till night'.[21] At the same tavern in 1662, Pepys dined by invitation with the 'officers of the Ordinance and other great persons and a very great dinner'.[22]

Much to the surprise of foreigners, taverns were also frequented by women, for '[o]ne might even believe that these houses are big brothels, did one not know the habits and customs of the country, because one always meets a great number of women there'.[23] Female proprietors, albeit often widows, were common. Women

24. *Still Life with bread, onion, herring and smoking accessories*, 1644. The redware brazier was used to light pipe tapers. Fish was widely eaten in taverns and inns during the 17th century. Pieter Claesz (1597-1660).

could and did dine in taverns without compromising their honour, and Mrs Pepys regularly met her husband and their friends for a meal at a favourite haunt. Nonetheless, the privacy of these rooms also enabled some to indulge in illicit affairs.

Taverns sold wine almost exclusively, and in prodigious amounts, to judge from the quantities held in the cellars. Average valuations for the stock are between £1,000 and £4,000 and, although the origin of the wine is rarely specified, by the end of the 17th century taverns and inns seem to be selling a greater proportion of French and Canary wine with relatively low amounts from the Rhineland, in spite of prohibitions on the importation of wines from France. Whilst the winestocks represented a considerable capital outlay, wine sales were the most profitable part of the business and a potential source of wealth for the proprietor. As the City of London Cash Accounts show, cellars were frequently extended to accommodate increasing demand for wine.[24] Alderman Abel of The Ship in Old Fish Street, noted for his wealth and vast stocks of wine, had to increase the size of his cellars, and his prosperity was emphasised in a contemporary broadside: 'he is now worth at least 10 or 12 thousand pounds,... his wives shoes must not now shine with the smeering and unsightly unguent of kitchen-stuffe; but the purest Black that Spaine affords [fine quality Spanish leather] must now cover her happy feet'.[25]

The English habit of drinking healths was remarked upon by a number of foreign visitors, who found the custom irksome. A meal was frequently interrupted in order to toast one's fellows, so that as French traveller Misson remarked, one has to sit a while with 'his Mouth cramm'd with a huge load of Victuals, which commonlly getting all to one side, raises the Cheek as high as an Egg…'.[26] Tudor and Stuart governments tried to control 'immoderate quaffing' in London through taxation and the regulation and licensing of outlets through which alcohol could be sold.[27] An Act of Parliament in 1553 limited the number of taverns in the City of London to forty. But by 1618, the Lord Mayor received a complaint that 'the City [had] within these few years become so pestered with taverns, that latterly the better sort of houses' had been acquired by vintners at unreasonable rents and converted 'to the maintenance of riot and disorder and the great inconvenience and disquiet of the neighbours'. Nonetheless, by 1633 the number had risen to 211, and by the end of the century tax assessments show that the proportion of officially licensed premises (including ale-houses) per household was one to thirteen and as much as one for every five households in certain areas of the City.[28] Until 1695 when the Justices of the Peace imposed a curfew of 10 pm in the winter and 11 pm in the summer, the only restriction on opening hours was closure during the Sabbath services.[29]

In the early 17th century there were several complaints that taverns had recently started a trade in victualling, selling more meat than the ordinaries and other eating-houses, which suggests a significant change in the function of these premises. Tavern keepers perhaps realised that they could attract more and higher spending customers by offering a wide range of food. Certainly by 1633, accounts suggest that 'as to victualling, there was scarce a tavern which did not most frequently use it'. Such diversification must also reflect demand and perhaps more businessmen required private dining facilities.[30] A greater choice of food was also offered in the ale-house by the end of the century and this was partly a response to the ever-rising demand for convivial, wholesome, cheap places to eat out; the collapse of the cooks' monopoly and increasing pressure on domestic living space and cooking facilities. As ale-houses became more respectable, their appeal widened to include customers from the middle and upper classes, for whom a breakfast draught of ale or a mid-morning snack was the first requirement of the day.[31]

The meals supplied by inns and taverns included food brought in by the patron to be cooked and consumed on the premises. There are several references to this custom in the Diaries of Pepys. On one occasion he purchased a lobster in Fish Street and, meeting friends with some sturgeon, they proceeded to the Sun Tavern to eat them.[32] Generally the food was supplied and cooked by the tavern, and meals varied from a simple dish of meat for one, to a venison pasty large enough to satisfy the healthy appetites of a several men over two days,[33] to a lavish feast or celebratory dinner for a party.[34] Treating the auditors of the Exchequer to a dinner at the Dolphin, Pepys and colleagues split the £5 6s between them, Pepys' share amounting to the substantial sum of 26s.[35]

25. Vintner and tavern proprietor Alderman William Abel and his wife Isabell were famed for their Friday night suppers at The Ship in Old Fish Street. Business boomed and the cellars were extended to accommodate demand.

Some taverns seem to have offered a limited range of food. To the consternation of Mr Talbot, who ate no fish, The Hoope tavern could offer nothing else, and a neat's (ox) tongue had to be sent for.[36] Others may have specialised. It is possible that The Ship tavern in Old Fish Street run by Alderman William Abel and his wife, Isabell, specialised in fish dishes, since they were famed for their Friday night suppers.[37]

Pepys provides some indication of the range of foods supplied by taverns, and he enjoyed poached eggs, ham, veal, bacon, powdered beef (sprinkled with salt and often stored in tubs in the cellars), steak, sausages, fritters, udder, neat's tongue, roasted meats including haunch of venison, chine of pork, shoulder of mutton, sirloin, capons and pullets, venison pasties, toasted and Whitsuntide cakes and codling (boiled apple) tarts. Large quantities of oysters were consumed and fish of all sorts including anchovies, ling, bloat-herrings and sturgeon. A useful indication of the quantity and range of food provided by taverns comes from the entertainment charges of the footmen, coachmen and others attending the King and Queen on Lord Mayor's Day. Distinguished guests and their retinues were usually entertained at local taverns. The bill from the Beare Inne in Bassishaw came to £21 for the provision and entertainment of 140 men, and included beef with vinegar, geese and pullets with sauce, custards and tarts, fruit and cheese, as well as 50 barrels of beer and ale. A charge of 6s was added to the bill for six bottles of claret for the Lords 'because the other Clarett was not liked'.[38] John Kilby of the White Lyon in Kings Street submitted his bill for £18 10s 4d, which included the loss of sixteen bottles; capers, samphire and four dishes of turnips; four legs of mutton; bread and beer; ten capons, a goose, three pieces of beef 'for ye 20 firstmen' (presumably those of higher office); and thirty bottles of claret, as well as a dinner for the Beadles, costing £2.[39]

The kitchens had to be sufficiently well equipped to cope with the relentless demand and some taverns and inns had two. They were always amply furnished with one or more ranges, four to ten spits, jacks, chains, irons and weights, gridirons, chopping boards, dripping pans, cleavers, toasting irons, chafing dishes, frying pans, kettles, skillets, saucepans, pestle and mortar, skimmers, stew pans and other vessels including fine and coarse pewter assessed by weight and often amounting to 900lbs or more; earthenware, wooden ware and usually a looking glass, sometimes a clock, cupboards, tables, stools and a bed. Occasionally one finds a reference to books and even muskets, bandoleers and swords.

Value for money aroused the same passions in the 16th and 17th centuries as it does today. In his *Penniless Pilgrimage*, John Taylor suggested that the proprietors of the Sun Taverns in London 'come upon a man with a ... bill as sharp cutting as a tailors...'.[40] Establishments serving meagre portions at high prices were frequently lampooned. The *nouvelle cuisine* in Locket's Tavern Charing Cross, was described by Lord Foppington as: 'much frequented by gentry, where you are so nicely served that, stap my vitals! they shall compose you a dish no bigger than a saucer which shall come to fifty shillings. In that eating-house, every fop with a small fortune who attempts to counterfeit quality is [a] fool...to bestow 20 shillings worth of sauce upon ten pennyworths of meat'.[41] Pepys describes one occasion, which fortunately turned to merriment, when with friends at the 'Sun Tavern in expectation of a dinner...we had sent us only two trencherfuls of meat...I winning a Quart of Sack...that one trencherful...was all lamb, and he that it was veale'.[42]

Sometimes the food was good but the accommodation poor. On 24 June 1663, the King's Head ordinary being full, Pepys went to another opposite, and whilst the proprietor was amiable and efficient and the food 'better than the other', the company and room were so small that Pepys felt the business would founder. Worst of all was the experience of bad food in insalubrious surroundings. On 23 January 1662 Pepys went with two friends to the Three Cranes Tavern and although they went to the 'best room in the house' it was such a 'narrow dogghole we were crammed (and I believe we were near 40) that it made me loathe my company and victuals, and a sorry poor dinner it was too'.[43]

Some taverns offered a fixed-price meal, or ordinary, equivalent to the modern *table d'hôte*. These were usually served at midday and offered seasonal fare. It seems from rather thin evidence that one and/or two courses were served, and beef dishes were especially popular. Prices varied considerably, ranging from 6d at the Black Eagle to as much as 2s 6d at the Blue Posts in Holborn. According to Thomas Dekker, 3d ordinaries attracted usurers, 'stale batchelors' and thrifty attorneys,[44] while Pontack's in Lombard Street, a noted ordinary 'for the better sort' and a celebrated French eating-house, charged 3s in 1690. Mr and Mrs Pepys attended the ordinary run by

Monsieur Robbins, a periwig-maker in Covent Garden, and spent 6s on a dinner served in the French manner, with three consecutive courses consisting of a mess of potage, *pigeons à l'esteuve* (stewed) and *boeuf-à-la-mode* (casserolled), all exceedingly well seasoned.[45] Some ordinaries were extremely pricy, and the eating-house in Spring Gardens charged 6s for a meal. It is unclear precisely when ordinaries were introduced, but the earliest references appear in the first decades of the 17th century. In contemporary legislation a distinction seems to have been made between tavern- and ordinary-keepers and keepers of ordinary tables. Some taverns clearly offered an ordinary in addition to their normal menus, possibly at special tables, but the term 'ordinary' also applied to a separate eating-house that offered nothing more than a fixed-price meal.[46] Pepys frequently dined at an ordinary, and he found them very convenient because 'a man knows what he hath to pay'. However, even the fixed price system caused problems on occassion, and at the ordinary opposite the Exchange, Pepys had a great wrangling with the master of the house when the reckoning was brought.[47] Perhaps it was for this reason that Pepys felt that the English could learn from the French and not consider it below a gentleman's dignity to bargain for his food before eating.[48] Pepys managed to obtain a meal for 12d at the fashionable King's Head ordinary by arriving late and having to sit at the second table.[49] But being late at the ordinary in the Old Exchange, he had to pay 18d, which was presumably, although he does not say so, also a reduction on the usual charge.[50]

COOKSHOPS – 'KITCHENS OF THE UNIVERSE'

The other specialised eating-house was the cookshop, which offered quick, hot meals as well as partly cooked and ready-to-eat convenience foods to take home.[51] Cookshop fare could also be brought into a tavern but had to be consumed by the purchaser and guests, because tavern-keepers were not permitted to offer cookshop food for re-sale.[52] By 1700 the cookshops had dispersed, with particular concentrations in the City centre and around the City gates.[53] This dispersal was partly due to the collapse of the cooks' monopoly and to ever-increasing demand for cheap, hot, fast foods from London's burgeoning and hungry population.

Many 17th-century accounts of cookshops conjure up an unsavoury picture of the food, hygiene and service provided.[54] In the *London Spy* published in 1698 Ned Ward visited the Giltspur Lane cookshops near Smithfield, 'the kitchen of the universe',[55] which specialised in pork dishes and catered for the market traders and visitors to the annual Bartholomew Fair held in August: '[a]t last…we gained Pie Corner, where Cooks stood dripping at their doors, like their roasted swines' flesh at their fires, each setting forth with an audible voice the choice and excellency of his pig and pork, which were running as merrily round the spit as if they were striving who should be first roasted.' Having selected an establishment, 'where we had great expectancy of tolerable meat and cleanly usage', Ward was rapidly disillusioned. The turnspit supervising the roasted swine 'rubbed his ears, breast, neck and arm-pits with the same wet cloth which he applied to his pigs'. A hoard of flies hovered over the pig-

26. Detail from David Tenier the Younger's *Kitchen Scene* (1644). The roasting range was the single most important piece of equipment in the cookshop kitchen.

sauce, and with a heaving stomach Ward took his leave.[56] Elsewhere, Ward refers to the 'measly pork and neck beef' disguised by carrots and marigold leaves available in Chick Lane and apparently consumed with relish by the carriers and drovers with 'fat [drivelling] down from the corners of their mouths'.[57] Cookshop pork is variously described by Ward as rotten, stinking and fly ridden. But is this image fair? After all, Ward writes with tongue in cheek, and as a tavern-keeper may have resented the thriving cookshop trade. Were cookshops cheap, greasy and nasty, frequented only by a coarse undiscerning public with desensitised nostrils and palates? It is difficult to determine the truth of the matter because the evidence is so partial. The problem is compounded because cookshops clearly catered for a wide market, but unlike the taverns and ordinaries some offered really cheap food for the poor. The quality of the establishment and the food provided was clearly variable. But the best seemed to specialise in roasted meats (poultry and game had to be ordered specially), beef, mutton, veal, pork and lamb. From these, Misson says you can have 'what quantity you please cut off, fat, lean, much or little done, with … a little salt and mustard upon the side of a plate…'.[58] Meals could cost as little as 8d and included a salad, a few vegetables, a bread roll and half a quart of beer.[59] By the end of the 17th century some cookshops seem to have specialised in selling chops, perhaps the precursor of the 18th-century chop house.[60]

The substantial kitchens usually contained a range or two, pot hangers, three or four spits,[61] bellows, numerous iron and copper cooking pots, warming pans, chafing

dishes, salt tubs, pestle and mortar, basting ladles, skillets, gridirons, scales and weights, dripping and frying pans, meat forks, fish plates and kettles, cleavers, chopping blocks and a spice box, with earthenware, glasses and fine and coarse pewter tableware. Beer and ale were stored in the cellar with extra pewter, coal, kindling and lumber. Inventories and Zetzner's reference to fish plates and kettles suggests that some cookshops provided fish dishes too.

London inventories[62] also show that the higher class cookshops had a specially designated dining room, often furnished with turkey-work upholstery, hangings, carpets and curtains. As Zetzner remarked, 'such a place is equally comfortable and useful to the middle classes and foreigners' for many London citizens did not have 'housekeeping arrangements at home, and [they] get what they require from the cookshop every day and thus economise. One meets important dealers, merchants and persons of quality and one is served on tablecloths and very white napkins'.[63] The economy spoke of here seems to refer to those who had a sufficiently large disposable income either to eat out by choice or to buy convenience foods to take home. But Pepys resorted to cookshop foods only when he had to; when the house was in disarray, if his kitchen servants were absent or if he needed to entertain. He dined in all types of venues during the early years of his Diary, but significantly ate at cookshops only four times up to 1665, twice to dine (with no further comment), once for a hasty meal 'where we ate a bit of mutton and away' and once because the preferred ordinary was full and after trying a few other places 'at last found some meat at a welch Cook's at Charing-Cross and there dined and our boys', which rather suggests a place of last resort.[64]

What then of the poor? Whilst Zetzner's comments about the lack of household arrangements applied to many Londoners who did not have their own kitchens, most had access to a hearth. Indeed, the vast quantity of ceramic cooking vessels with sooted bases and tripod feet recovered from excavations in London testify to widespread domestic hearth cooking in this period. But the poor also supplemented their pot-based cuisine with food from the hucksters (street sellers), with bakemeats from the bakehouse and from the lower-class cookshops selling cheap cuts of meat, sausages, offal, small beer and bread.[65]

PLEASURE GARDENS – DINING *AL FRESCO*

Whenever they had leisure and opportunity, Londoners enjoyed the pleasures of eating out of doors, escaping across the river to 'wild areas and pleasure grounds' and into the fields to the north of the City.[66] Those with means obtained the lease or

27. London's first floating coffee-house serving light refreshments opened in the early 1660s. Moored off Cuper's Stairs, Southwark, it was notorious for gambling and prostitution.

purchase of 'faire garden plots and summer houses for pleasure', and a number of these dwellings can be seen on a c.1559 picture map of London in Cripplegate Ward and Finsbury Fields.[67] By the early 1600s Pleasure Gardens were fashionable, and eating-houses with large gardens were developed on the sites of mineral springs surrounding the capital. The favourites were those of Spring Gardens near Charing Cross, and from 1661 the New Spring Gardens (Vauxhall) and Cuper's Gardens on the South Bank. But the eating-house at Vauxhall was expensive and most of the people who thronged the paths and arbours on fair spring and summer evenings probably made do with light refreshments of syllabub or cake.

Meals were probably available in The Folly, a floating barge, moored by Cuper's or Cupid's Stairs, where visitors to the gardens landed. This 'whimsical piece of architecture', and den of iniquity, was designed as 'a musical summer-house for the entertainment of quality, where they might meet and ogle one another…but the ladies of the town finding it as convenient a rendezvous for their purposes, dash'd the female quality out of countenance and made them seek a more retired conveniency for their amorous intrigues'.[68] There were small compartments for private parties and the deck afforded an open area for promenade. Inside, burnt brandy and other drinks were offered at the bar.

Within the gardens at Charing Cross were common bowling greens and an expensive ordinary charging as much as 6s per meal. By 1634 the gardens had 'grown scandalous and insufferable…with continual bibbing and drinking wine all day under the trees [and] two or three quarrel every week'.[69] Thereafter, a new Spring Garden was established in the fields behind, with a 'fair house', called Shaver's Hall, to entertain 'gamesters and bowlers at excessive rates'.[70] The gardens of Shaver's Hall covered three acres, with gravel walks, arbours, bowling alleys, orchards and facilities for dining and banqueting.

COFFEE-HOUSES AND CHOCOLATE-HOUSES – 'OUTLANDISH DRINKS'

'These houses, which are very numerous in London, are extremely convenient. You have all Manner of News there;…a good fire, which you may sit by as long as you please; You have a Dish of Coffee; you meet your Friends for the transaction of business and all for a Penny, if you don't care to spend more'.[71] Contemporary writers such as Mission stressed that coffee-houses were frequented by all classes of society, apart from the poor, some claiming that they were the resort of tradesmen who frittered away time instead of working, others that they were venues for the idle and disaffected, a potential breeding ground of sedition.[72] Notwithstanding the coffee-house developed a major role as the focus for information exchange in London's economic and social life.

In the 17th century, coffee-houses concentrated solely on the liquid refreshment trade, offering no sustenance beyond a morsel of biscuit to accompany a drink. The first London coffee-house was established in 1652 by Pasqua Rosee in St Michael's Alley, Cornhill; his advertisement extols the virtues of the drink that must 'be taken as

Overleaf
28. A London Coffee House, signed and dated A.S. 1668.

hot as possibly can be endured the which will never fetch the skin off the mouth, or raise any Blisters, by reason of that Heat'.[73] Coffee was good for the eyes, 'and the better if you hold your Head over it, and take in the Steem that way', and it would 'prevent Drowsiness, and make one fit for business'.[74]

Even though it was regarded as an 'outlandish drink',[75] coffee-houses sprang up throughout the metropolis. By 1663 there were 83 in the City alone, with particular concentrations in Broadstreet, Farringdon without and Cornhill wards frequented by the business community.[76] The demand was such that many victualling houses and private dwellings were converted to coffee-houses, sometimes to the inconvenience and alarm of those nearby. The neighbours of barber and coffee-house proprietor James Farr were annoyed by 'evil smells and for keeping of ffier night and day whereby his chimney and chambers hath been sett on fire'.[77]

The licences of the coffee-house proprietors[78] show that a range of beverages were offered, including chocolate; with lemon-, rose- and violet-perfumed sherbets; mineral waters; and tea.[79] A substantial proportion of coffee-house proprietors also held liquor licences, providing quality wines, cordials, beer, ale and spirits.[80] Competition between coffee-house keepers was intense, and most vied with each other to offer a distinctive and wide range of good quality, freshly prepared beverages which invariably included a brand of punch unique to the house.[81] To boost trade many proprietors sold raw or partly processed beans, tea, tobacco and bottled drinks, so that it is sometimes difficult to differentiate between those who sold goods wholesale and those who made up the drinks on site.

Customers were attracted to the coffee-houses by the smell of 'burnt Crust'[82], by the exotic imagery of the signs (a Turk, Sultan or Mogul resplendent in turban, or a Turkish pot and coffee cup) and at night by the brilliantly illuminated entrance. Much space was taken up by the coffee-room or rooms on the ground and/or first floor,[83] and some indication of their appearance can be gleaned from inventories and

29. A selection of coffee and chocolate cups in tin-glazed earthenware, 17th century. There is a Turk's head design inside one of the bowls. Coffee was known as the 'turkish berry', and the Turk's Head was a popular name for a coffee-house.

the few images which have survived. Most had large sash windows set high in walls lined with panels of deal adorned with 'gilt Frames containing an abundance of Rarieties…'.[84] To one side stood a boxed booth or bar, often with a canopy. The coffee-rooms were simply furnished with tables, stools, benches and in the grander establishments with leather upholstered chairs.[85] A large fire and grate supported a cistern or boiler, with an iron to roast the beans and keep the brass and pewter coffee and chocolate pots warm. Closets contained a supply of glasses, drinking vessels, scales and weights, candlesticks, tobacco pipes and other supplies.[86] The drink ingredients were stored and often partly prepared in the cellars and garrets.[87] Coffee-houses were open from 6 am until late at night, but the busiest periods seem to have been from 10 am till noon, after dinner from 4 until 6 pm, then again from 8 till 10 pm. No liquor could be sold after 10 pm.[88]

English coffee-houses, unlike their continental counterparts, were solely for men. Women clearly purchased coffee, chocolate and tea for domestic consumption, but do not seem to have frequented coffee-houses as customers.[89] Nevertheless, a high percentage of coffee-houses were run by women during this period, and female servants may have been employed, but they probably served behind the bar, leaving the pot-boys to wait on the clients.[90] It has been suggested that the word 'tip' (in the sense of a gratuity) originated in the 17th-century coffee-house as an acronym for 'To Insure Promptness', customers placing their money in a special box on the bar.[91]

The price of a dish of coffee remained fairly stable until the early 18th century, when The Postman claimed that the majority of retailers then charged 1½d per dish and 'that no person that sells Coffee for 1d a Dish can make good Coffee'.[92] From the 1650s a little dish of coffee 'with or without sugar' usually cost 1d and came with a tobacco-filled pipe. Coffee with milk cost 1 1/2d plus a piece of biscuit. Milk, added to tea and coffee, seems to have become more popular towards the end of the 17th century. Chocolate was regarded as a nourishing breakfast drink, but was much more expensive, a large cup, which included egg yolks, milk and a little sugar, costing 4d.[93]

30. Part of a coffee-house tile panel inscribed 'DISH OF COFFEE BOY', from Baxter's Coffee Rooms, 66 Brick Lane. Early 18th century.

Focus Drinking and Toasting Lucy Peltz

From the late 17th century, coffee-houses and taverns shaped masculine social life in London. They were places where men went to chat, read newspapers and to drink. Some thought such company was rather too inclusive so clubs were established, often in the private rooms of the same London taverns, where elected members met to discuss a variety of topics including science, literature and the arts.

One of the most famous was the Kit cat Club, founded in the 1680s, which took its name from Christopher Cat, a mutton pie-maker and proprietor of the Cat and Fiddle, in Gray's Inn Lane, where they first met. Another was the Society of Dilettanti, which began in 1732 as a dining club for gentlemen who had made the Grand Tour to Italy. Both provided a convivial setting where elected members, regardless of rank, could

meet for mutual support and conversation on matters of common interest and current affairs. Such gentlemen's clubs approved of wine as a social lubricant; the author Samuel Johnson believed that 'moderate drinking' improved the quality of conversation by 'making people talk better'.[94] Despite the Kit Kat's patronage of such playwrights as Congreve and Dryden, which established their reputation for cultured discourse and politeness, their meetings may not have been so refined; members consumed around '20 gallons of claret, 6 of canary…4 of white wine' at one meeting in 1689![95]

Much of the wine drunk at such clubs at the start of the 18th century would have been imbibed in the widespread and noisy process of drinking repeated 'healths', or toasts, to absent friends, the monarch and the present company. It is a happy

Above left
31. In Sir Joshua Reynold's group portrait of the Society of Dilettanti (1779), members toast Sir William Hamilton's new publication on ancient vases (Society of Dilettanti).

Above
32.a,b William Hogarth's engraving *A Midnight Modern Conversation* (1732–33) shows a group of drunken men at the end of a night of hard drinking at St John's coffee-house, Shire Lane, Temple Bar. It was so popular that its motifs appear on a variety of objects including this white salt glazed mug (*c.*1733).

coincidence that English baluster and 'firing' glasses were manufactured with heavy 'feet' that could withstand being 'hammered' down on the table when the drinker responded to the toast. Indeed, a sense of the ambience of toasting is revealed in a range of glasses, including deceptive ones for cautious toast-masters that appeared full when only containing the smallest measure or those engraved with commemorative toasts like the 'Houghton Goblet'.

Though Englishmen have ever been proud of the quantities they drink, the visible excess of drunkenness became increasingly unacceptable as the 18th century progressed. This paradox was captured in Hogarth's enormously successful *A Midnight Modern Conversation*, whose various motifs of masculine intemperance satirised the inevitable upshot of a night spent drinking punch. The evils of drink might not be so apparent in a wax sculpture of Samuel Johnson's Literary Club, but one contemporary source appears to have interpreted this work as the 'progress of inebriety'.[96] Among chosen friends, and in the private rooms of the Turk's Head Tavern, even public figures like James Boswell, Charles James Fox, Reynolds and Thomas Gainsborough were not above an evening's over-indulgence in the bottle.

Left
33. Wax model of Samuel Johnson's Literary Club (*c.*1790) attributed to Samuel Percy, depicting a high-spirited meeting at the Turk's Head Tavern. The company shown includes Samuel Johnson, Sir Joshua Reynolds, Thomas Gainsborough, Topham Beauclerk, Charles James Fox, James Boswell and Joseph Nollekens.

Far Left
34. A selection of decorated 18th-century baluster and toasting glasses from the Garton Collection in the Museum of London. The celebrated lead glass 'Houghton goblet' was probably made for Sir Robert Walpole to commemorate the building of Houghton, his mansion in Norfolk; it is inscribed 'Fari quae Sentio. Prosperity to Houghton'.

18th century

Edwina Ehrman

New money and a new emphasis on pleasure increased spending on eating out in the 18th century. Economic prosperity stimulated the growth of the middleclass creating an important group of consumers, who were eager to advance their position in society and embrace the lifestyle of their social superiors. To fulfill their ambitions they spent money on fashion, leisure and entertainment. In this competitive environment where 'seeing and being seen' was all-important eating out assumed a new significance.

Inn-holders and victuallers quickly realised the moneymaking potential of this sizeable group of consumers and tried to attract their patronage by offering experiences to match their social and material aspirations. At nearly all the venues competition for customers was intense. It was vital to project the name of one's garden or tavern or coffee-house into the public consciousness. Print was a powerful weapon in the battle to win business. Proprietors advertised at every opportunity and paid for editorial puffs. They stressed the polite and attentive service, the genteel accommodation, and the novelty and fashion of the fixtures and fittings. The excellence of the larder, the quality of the cellar and specialities of the house, like whitebait and turtle, were described in glowing terms. Dinners could be dressed 'on the shortest notice', and parties were always catered for on liberal terms. For the first time recipe books were published by tavern and coffee-house owners and cooks. Landlords made the maximum use of their premises and developed their services both to maintain their core customers and to attract passing trade.

In seeking to enter the fashionable world and so move above their 'natural' station in life the newly affluent exposed themselves to the ridicule of satirists and the disapproval of moralists. The author of *The Art of Living in London*[1] highlights the temptations of luxury eating, a habit that robs its victims of time and money – vital commodities in a city that thrived on commerce. He warns against being seduced by the choice food, leisured service and comforts of the inn. The mouth-watering displays of early fruit and vegetables, melons, cucumbers and young peas add unexpected costs to the bill of even a modest establishment. Like many similar 18th-century 'guides' to London the author professes to address the young, inexperienced visitor unprepared for the city's temptations and in need of a mentor.

35. The officer is eating a syllabub. Made from wine and milk or cream, the liquid was drunk and the whipped cream floating on top eaten with a spoon (*The Pretty Barmaid* after John Collett, 1770).

INNS, TAVERNS AND CHOP HOUSES

Visitors who travelled to London by coach were set down at inns, which offered a full range of services including accommodation, light refreshments, meals and stabling. The best were comfortably and fashionably furnished to attract the patronage of the wealthiest classes. The Saracen's Head in Friday Street, described by John Strype[2] in 1720 as 'very large and of a great Resort and Trade', served routes to and from Dorset and the West Country. An inventory of 1719[3] reveals that it had at least thirty-four well-appointed guestrooms and two suites, all furnished with tables and chairs so that meals could be eaten in privacy. The public areas included a parlour and hall. The parlour, furnished both for taking tea and eating, was decorated with many homely and genteel touches. It had two birdcages, a corner cupboard decorated with a display of china, ornaments on the chimneypiece and a writing desk. Typically the walls were hung with a looking glass, clock, map and prints. Tea, coffee and chocolate, wine, beer and punch were available. Meals were prepared in the well-equipped kitchen. Roast, grilled, fried, stewed and boiled food could all be provided together with pasties, pies and toasted cheese. The thirty-six knives and forks listed in the inventory suggest the maximum number the inn could cater for at one time. Some guests, however, may have used their own travelling sets of cutlery. There were many pewter plates and a few pewter drinking vessels as well as pieces made from less durable but more decorative, and costly, materials such as glass, delftware and china. Imported Chinese porcelain, the most appropriate and up-to-date material from which to drink tea, was provided in the parlour and withdrawing room of the most lavishly decorated suite.

The hall was sparsely furnished with three large tables and twenty-one cane chairs, relieved only by a couple of turkey-work carpets. The hall was for the carrying trade and budget traveller, while the parlour was reserved for more affluent guests. Its

36. Ceramic vessels (c.1750–90) found on the site of the King's Arms Inn in Uxbridge, Middlesex. The creamware pieces include a well made sauceboat, mustard pot and cover and a salt cellar. Chinese porcelain (left) and some fashionable English Worcester tea wares (right) were also recovered.

attractive fixtures and fittings, although perhaps not of the quality they were used to, would reassure them of the high standards of The Saracen's Head, the good taste of their host and his understanding of their needs.

The continuing use of better quality ceramics alongside everyday ware is also illustrated by late 18th-century finds from the site of the former King's Arms Inn in Uxbridge, Middlesex. Here a large quantity of broken pottery and glass recovered from a cistern included many well-used, functional creamware plates and several more decorative and finely potted pieces, including Chinese porcelain and fashionable Worcester porcelain tea wares. As at The Saracen's Head, the landlord provided standard dinner service wares for general use and better quality pieces for his more select guests.[4]

Taverns also offered accommodation and dining facilities but, unlike inns, the majority of their customers were male. Traditionally only wine was sold, but in the 18th century they broadened their appeal and increasingly served beer and spirits. Private rooms were available for dining, as well as for clubs, societies and business meetings. The larger establishments offered dinner, eaten as the main meal in the early part of the afternoon, and an evening service. Customers could order meals of their choice in advance. Those taverns that did not offer supper usually welcomed the services of itinerant street sellers who hawked pies and other fast foods. Oyster and shrimp girls often took up a stand at the door of smaller taverns and ale-houses. Landlords had little objection to the sale of salty snacks, which encouraged liquor sales, the source of the bulk of their profits.

Some taverns were known for their food, and their cooks published recipe books for home use. In 1773 John Townshend, who described himself 'Late Master of the Greyhound Tavern, Greenwich, and Cook to his Grace the Duke of Manchester', published *The Universal Cook; or lady's complete assistant*. This was followed in 1788 by *The English Art of Cookery* by Richard Briggs, 'many years Cook at the White-Hart Tavern, Holborn: Temple Coffee-House, and other Taverns in London' and four years later by Francis Collingwood and John Woollams' *The Universal Cook and city and Country Housekeeper*. They are thought to have been cooks at the Crown and Anchor tavern in the Strand, which was known for the size of its ballroom. In 1798, 2,000 people were entertained at the tavern in honour of Charles James Fox's birthday.[5] Dr Campbell, who visited London from Ireland in 1775 to meet Dr Johnson, was put out by the cost of a meal at the Crown and Anchor. His party was charged £3 10s for 'a pound of cod &c'. He particularly regretted a fellow diner's pretension in ordering 'a shrimp sauce &c'.[6]

Perhaps the best-known cookery book associated with a tavern is John Farley's *The London Art of Cookery* published in 1783. John Farley was the principal cook at The London Tavern in Bishopsgate Street, which had an unrivalled reputation for its cooking at the end of the 18th century. William Hickey wrote in his *Memoirs* that it 'surpassed every other tavern we went to. The dinner excellent, served in a style of magnificence peculiar to that house, wines all of the best'.[7] Roach's *London Pocket*

Pilot of 1793 also recommended it: 'At this house are to be met all the most delicate luxuries upon earth'. Tantalisingly, there seems to be no details of meals. Farley's cookery book, which provides a record of recipes current at the time, was in fact ghost written by Richard Johnson, a hack writer, who was paid £21 for his work.[8] The recipes were plagiarised from previously published books, a common practice then as now. It was written 'for the Use of all Ranks in general' with recipes suitable for 'either the Peer or the Mechanic'.[9] This egalitarian approach reflects the political climate of the time. The tavern was a meeting place for the Supporters of the Bill of Rights who had backed the American colonists in their fight for independence, which was won in 1783, the year the book was published.

Many eating-houses, including taverns, continued to offer a fixed-price meal at a fixed hour. The time of the ordinary depended on the location of the eating-house and the clientele. Having risen early, artisan and working men dined at noon. Those who did business at the Royal Exchange in the City looked for an ordinary after its doors closed at three o'clock. Ordinaries were particularly popular on Sundays with families and city dwellers who wanted a day out in the rural areas that encircled the urban centre.

Following the custom at the time, all the dishes making up the single-course meal were placed on the table at once. Although waiters were on hand to pass plates, the person nearest a dish was expected to carve and serve everyone. Satirical prints and writings of the period often portray a chaotic scene with some diners tucking in, studiously ignoring their fellows, whilst others fight over the food. The author of The Art of Living in London advises his reader to reserve his place with an inverted plate at the end of the table nearest the serving mat. He can then pile his own plate high with meat and pudding as soon as it appears on the table.[10] Similar advice was given over 200 years later by the restaurant critic Lt-Col. Newnham-Davis. Sensuously describing the pleasures of the pudding served at the Cheshire Cheese in Fleet Street, he wrote: 'The man who loves the Cheshire Cheese pudding is in his place at table a few minutes before the pudding is brought in at 6.30 P.M., a surging billow of creamy white bulging out of a great brown bowl…'.[11]

Some taverns and eating-houses in the centre tried to increase Sunday custom by providing a free cold lunch, a convenient way of using leftovers. Not surprisingly the meals were considered poor, but wine sales were good. Francis Place recorded how he economised, whilst a journeyman breeches-maker, by eating the cheaper, cold food offered for dinner at a public house in the Strand. He was perfectly satisfied with his meal of meat and bread washed down with a pint of porter, which he described as being quite enough for a hearty man's dinner. The total cost was 6 ¾d.[12] Taverns and public houses also offered cold food for supper together with light hot dishes such as poached eggs and toasted cheese.

Experiences of eating out can be culled from the letters and diaries of visitors to London. James Boswell lived in lodgings in Downing Street and although he was able to dine with his landlord's family whenever he liked for 1s a time he often preferred

37. Middle-class families sometimes enjoyed a meal out on Sundays at one of the many taverns that offered a fixed price meal or 'ordinary' (Detail from *A Hen-pecked Husband* after Thomas Rowlandson, post 1866).

to eat out. In his *London Journal*, written in 1762–63, he mentions a number of eating places including taverns and eating-houses but seems to have particularly liked Clifton's Chop House in Butcher Row, which he describes as 'a very good chop house'. The fast service offered by chop houses made them a popular choice in a city known for its bustle and hurrying inhabitants. The range of food, and a hint of other attractions, is conveyed in an anonymous poem of 1750 in praise of 'Pretty Sally of the Chop House':[13]

> Dear Sally, emblem of thy chop-house ware.
> As broth reviving, and as white bread fair,
> As small beer grateful and as pepper strong;
> As beef stake tender, as fresh as pot herbs young
> As sharp as a knife, and as piercing as a fork-
> Soft as new butter, white as fairest pork;
> Sweet as young mutton, brisk as bottled beer;
> Smooth as oil, juicy as cucumber,
> As bright as cruet void of vinegar.

Chop houses were generally furnished with boxes and either wooden or curtained partitions and bench seating. The tables were covered with white cloths and set with cruets and salts. Hooks were provided for hats, and the ubiquitous clock hung on the wall, sometimes accompanied by prints or a looking glass. Contemporary images show them crowded with men and seething with activity. Several London chop houses survived into the 20th century with their layout hardly changed over two centuries.

Another London venue favoured by Boswell was Dolly's in Paternoster Row, near St Paul's Cathedral. It is described both as a chop house and a beef-steak house but Boswell enjoyed its juicy steaks. The author of *The Art of Living in London* also dwells nostalgically on the perfect steak, which he recommended should be eaten with either York or Burton ale. Regional beers, although significantly more costly than London brewed beers, were popular in the capital. In 1712 Burton ale was advertised in London for 7s 6d per dozen bottles and by 1722 more than 1,000 barrels a year were shipped to London from Hull. There was a growing preference too for strong, highly malted beers. Porter, a dark beer similar to stout, which was produced by a number of London brewers from the 1720s, met this taste at a reasonable price. In 1736 labourers were said to drink about four pints of strong beer a day.[14]

ALE-HOUSES, STREET FOOD AND COOKSHOPS

Working men drank in ale-houses, which were increasingly known as public houses. They offered bread, cheese and buns and some would cook a customer's own food or prepare a meal by prior arrangement. By the end of the century many provided ordinaries and a hot midday meal. Like taverns, they offered credit, which was an added incentive to spend. The scores were chalked up and debts called in on Saturday night when wages were paid. In the 18th century ale-houses became better regulated and more respectable. The more enterprising and progressive victuallers invested money in upgrading fixtures and fittings in line with those in taverns and inns. Most houses had a taproom and a parlour with more comfortable seating and a quieter environment. Upstairs rooms were made available for clubs and meetings. Outside, some landlords set up skittle and bowling alleys. These improved facilities naturally attracted more reputable and well-to-do customers, and shopkeepers and tradesmen frequented the better ale-houses. Many ale-houses, however, still provided basic facilities in cramped surroundings for customers who either could not afford better or did not wish to.

Bread and cheese were the main constituents of the diet of the poor, particularly in the country. The urban poor had access to a larger range of cheap food sold in markets and on the street. For centuries street sellers had taken up a stand or walked the main thoroughfares crying their wares. Puddings and pies were sold from barrows with a heated compartment and women fried sausages for

customers who sat on stools enjoying the warmth of the brazier. Sausages and hot spiced gingerbread cut into shapes and sometimes gilded were popular with children. Some street sellers baked their own pies, puddings and cakes, others used the facilities of a local baker to bake the ingredients they had prepared, or sold on the baker's behalf.[15] Not all street food was sold to the poor. Oyster girls in particular attracted more affluent clients. Contemporary prints and ballads often allude to the physical charms of the oyster girls, and by extension to the aphrodisiac qualities of oysters. Young rakes visiting their mistresses were advised to give 'Nature a Fill-up with Wine, Jellies, Oysters, and other Provocatives'.[16] The prints also show the girls fending off the unwanted attentions of tavern drunks.

Many poor London families lived in one room in multiple occupancy housing. If they had a fireplace at all it was not constructed for efficient cooking, and fuel was

38. The pudding seller's barrow probably contained a firebox to burn charcoal to keep his puddings hot. A harness attached the handles of the barrow to his body leaving him free to serve customers (*Hot Pudding Seller* by Paul Sandby, 1759).

costly. Most could only afford the most essential cooking vessels, the most important being a kettle. Irregular funds and lack of storage space also meant that ingredients had to be purchased in small quantities from the chandler, the 18th-century equivalent of the all-purpose corner shop. Furthermore, many working women employed outside the home would have had neither the time nor energy to prepare food. A pie or joint could be cooked at the local baker's for a small fee, but an alternative was to collect a takeaway from a cook-shop or eat there.

Most 18th-century writers, following Ned Ward, describe the food offered in cookshops as unappetising, if not repulsive: 'Measly Pork, rusty Bacon, stinking Lamb, rotten Mutton, slinked Veal, and Coddled Cow, with yellow Greens, sooty Pottage, and greasy Pudding, sold at the Common Cooks Shops about the Skirts of the Town'.[17] Smollet's Roderick Random describes the physical location and atmosphere of a typical cookshop. In a basement room, he found himself 'in the middle of a cook's shop, almost suffocated with the steam of boiled beef, and surrounded by a company consisting chiefly of hackney coachmen, chairmen, draymen, and a few footmen out of place, or on board wages, who sat eating shin-of-beef, tripe, cow-heel, or sausages, at separate boards, covered with cloths which turned my stomach.'[18]

CONFECTIONERS, TURTLE AND SOUP

Syllabubs, jellies, sweets and pastries could be eaten at the counter of London confectioners. Georg Christoph Lichtenberg described their temptations to a friend in Göttingen in a letter written in April 1770.

'The confectioners dazzle your eyes with their candelabra and tickle your nose with their wares for no more trouble and expense than that of taking both into their establishments. In these hang festoons of Spanish grapes, alternating with pineapples, and pyramids of apples and oranges, among which hover attendant white-armed nymphs with silk caps and little silk trains…'.[19]

Gilray and other artists visualised these pleasures in social satires like *Hero's recruiting at Kelsey's*. Using light to entice customers into shops was not new. Defoe criticised the money lavished on fitting out a pastry-cook's shop with lights, mirrors and silver in 1710. Thomas Carter's shop in St Bride's in the 1730s was more modest, but he sold an impressive range of confectionery, retail and wholesale.[20] Customers could buy ratafia and heart cakes, macaroons, gingerbread nuts, lemon biscuits, sponge biscuits, jumballs and knotts. For the sweet-toothed there were candied, dried and preserved fruits, wet and dry sweetmeats, varieties of comfits including cardamom, sugar roses, barley sugar and chocolate drops.[21]

Confectioners were regarded as the most skilled members of their profession and ranked among the most respectable tradesmen. The most successful, who combined culinary expertise and business skills, made a handsome living. They needed capital to equip their shop and kitchens, employ staff and buy in expensive imported raw ingredients, and social skills to attract the most discriminating clients. Confectioners are the only food professionals to be listed in *The Universal Director* of 1763.[22]

39. London confectioners were noted for their tempting displays of preserved fruits, jellies and sweets. Here Captain Birch and his companion are enjoying syllabubs and sugar plums (dragees) at Kelsey's in St James's Street (*Hero's Recruiting at Kelsey's or – Guard-Day at St James's* by James Gilray, 1797).

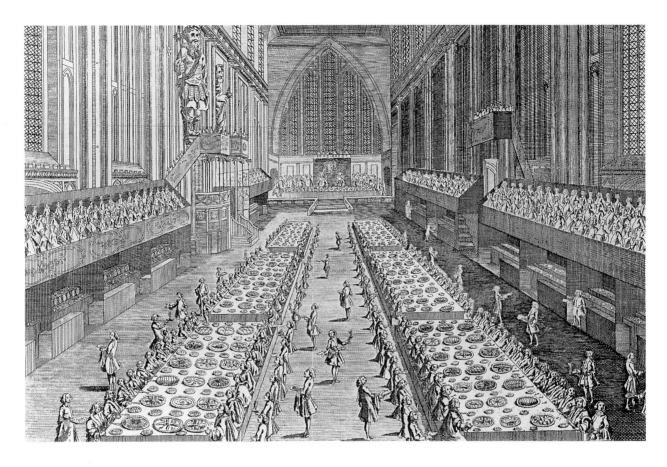

40. An engraving of the 1761 banquet given by the Lord Mayor and attended by George III and Queen Charlotte, showing the tables set *à la Française*. The king and queen are seated at the high table (A View of the inside of Guildhall as it appear'd on Lord Mayor's Day, 1761, *Gentleman's Magazine*, December 1761).

Three, Frederick Kuhff, Confectioner to His Majesty, Jeremiah Wilder and James Scott, played an important part in the preparations for a banquet given by the Lord Mayor in the Guildhall, and attended by King George III and Queen Charlotte, on Lord Mayor's Day in 1761. Over 1,200 people were present, and 729 attendants and servants of the royal party were entertained in the neighbourhood. The total cost of the evening, including wine and food, the erection and equipment of a temporary kitchen, hire charges, interior decorations, lighting, staff, musicians and security, was £1605 7s 6d.

Five cooks supervised the work in the kitchen and the king's cook oversaw the dishes prepared for him. Four courses were served to the king's table. The other tables had only one course consisting of a selection of the dishes offered to the king chosen according to the rank of the guests. The dishes for the first course were placed on the table before the guests sat down in a balanced arrangement in accordance with the conventions of the *service à la Française*, which directed which types of dishes should be placed at the ends, sides, corners and centre. After the covers had been removed, the soup and fish were eaten first and their places filled by meat dishes. The first course included roast venison and turtle, both high-status foods, and many meat dishes such as *tongues Espagniole*, *chicken a la Reine* and *fillets of mutton a la Memorance*. Thirty-two dishes of 'fine vegetables' accompanied the meats. The second course

consisted of game – ortolans, pea-chicks, wheatears, teal, snipe and woodcocks. This was followed by a course of lighter meat and vegetable dishes, including a dish of duck's tongues, three of 'fine fat livers', *a ragout royal*, ten dishes of fine green peas, five of *artichoaks a la Provincale* and a dish of *cardoons a la Bejamel*. The menu combined English and French styles of cooking with many elaborate 'made-dishes' alongside traditional English roasts.

The dessert course was designed to demonstrate the skills of the pastry cook and confectioner. Dishes of 'fine cut pastry' and 'blomanges representing different figures' were set alongside 'curious ornamented cakes'. The King's table alone was decorated with a centrepiece. A 'Grand Pyramid' of shellfish was flanked by two 'Grand Epergnes fill'd with fine Pickles & Garnish'd round with Plates of Sorts…'. Jellies made to look like landscapes, temples and other 'shapes', together with savoury cakes and almond 'g[r]ottoes', were arranged around them.[23] These set pieces provided a visual climax to the table and a topic of conversation. Novelty shapes made from jelly were an 18th-century conceit, while those made from blancmange had been a talking point since Tudor times.[24]

The turtle served on the king's and three other tables at the 1761 banquet was a recent introduction. There is an early reference to it in the fourth edition of Hannah Glasse's *The Art of Cookery made Plain and Easy* published in 1751. The additions

41.a,b One of a pair of Chinese export porcelain punch bowls presented to the Worshipful Company of Cooks in 1799. It is decorated with the company's arms and trophies of game. A turtle, which was a new food in England in the 18th century, is enamelled inside the bowl.

42. A view of Vauxhall Gardens showing some of the supper boxes on the left. Other people sit beneath the orchestra. Simple cold food was served and a range of wines, table beer and cider. (*Vauxhall Gardens, shewing the Grand Walk*, by J.S. Muller after S. Wale, 1751).

include instructions on how 'To Dress a Turtle, the West-India Way', starting with how it should be killed.[25] Two years later the *Gentleman's Magazine* included an account of the difficulties in cooking a turtle at the King's Arms Tavern in Pall Mall. It was so large (159kg) that the door of the oven had to be taken off. As the century progressed, taverns and coffee-houses, which were now serving full meals, frequently advertised turtle in the newspapers. They were captured in the West Indies and the Ascension Islands and transported live to England. Several taverns including the London Tavern and the Shakespeare's Head in Covent Garden were famous for their tanks of live turtles. Bones from the green and other edible turtles showing evidence of butchery continue to be found in excavations in London.[26] Several dishes were made from the flesh and inner parts, but the most popular was soup. Those who could not afford real turtle made do with mock turtle made from a calf's head stewed in Madeira and a rich meat broth well flavoured with herbs and spices. Birch and Birch, pastry cooks, confectioners and caterers, of 15 Cornhill, sold both turtle and mock turtle. The comparative costs are revealed in the firm's daybooks. In November 1776 they supplied terrines of mock turtle at 5s each and of real turtle at 12s 6s.[27]

Soup was eaten in the 18th century both as part of the first course of dinner and as a light meal. Towards the end of the century it was offered by some confectioners' shops and was recommended for people with weak stomachs and poor digestion as well as for hangovers.

Let a good soup, these days, your dinner be;

Your health 'twill serve – 'twill serve frugality.[28]

It was also regarded as a restorative in France. The word 'restaurant' first appeared in the 16th century meaning any food that restores, but it came to be used more specifically to describe particularly reviving soup. By 1771 the definition also included 'an establishment specialising in the sale of restorative foods'. Six years earlier a bouillon-seller in Paris called Boulanger had opened a soup room, which he advertised as selling 'restoratives fit for the gods'. He implored: 'Come unto me, all you whose stomachs are aching, and I will restore you'.[29] In London, Mr Horton, a confectioner, set up a soup room in Cornhill, which offered a fashionable dining experience in the latest French style. An engraving of about 1770 shows an elegant vaulted room hung with Venetian mirrors and stucco swags. Men and women chat over light refreshments.[30] By the 19th century the term 'restaurant' had taken on its current meaning of a place offering professionally cooked food in an elegant environment with either an *à la carte* or *table d'hôte* menu.[31]

PLEASURE GARDENS AND TEA GARDENS

The eating places described so far were almost entirely frequented by men. Prostitutes haunted the less reputable ones, but respectable women are rarely mentioned. At the end of the century John Britton records occasionally meeting women at the modest eating-house in Holborn where he dined.[32] Earlier Dr Johnson and the Ivy-lane Club had entertained Charlotte Lennox, her husband and a woman friend to a bohemian supper at the Devil Tavern in Fleet Street; the party went on all night and was probably an exceptional occasion.[33] The social life of genteel women was focused in the home with occasional visits to assembly rooms and routs, while men pursued their friendships and interests outside in coffee-houses, taverns and chop houses. In the summer, however, women were able to enjoy eating out at London's many tea and pleasure gardens.

In the 18th century Spring Gardens was developed by its owner Jonathan Tyers into an entertainment complex, offering the public an escapist, pleasure-filled evening. Its successful formula, which combined music, illuminations, fireworks and light refreshments in a fairy-tale setting, was widely copied. Tyers stage-managed the evening's events with theatrical flair. One of his special effects is described in *England's Gazeteer* of 1751: 'Here are fine pavilions, shady groves, and the most delightful walks, illuminated by above one thousand lamps, so disposed that they all take fire together, almost as quick as lightning, and dart such a sudden blaze as is perfectly surprising'. Another surprise was the emergence of the paintings that decorated the supper boxes, which suddenly appeared at a fixed time.[34] The gardens offered an *à la carte* menu of

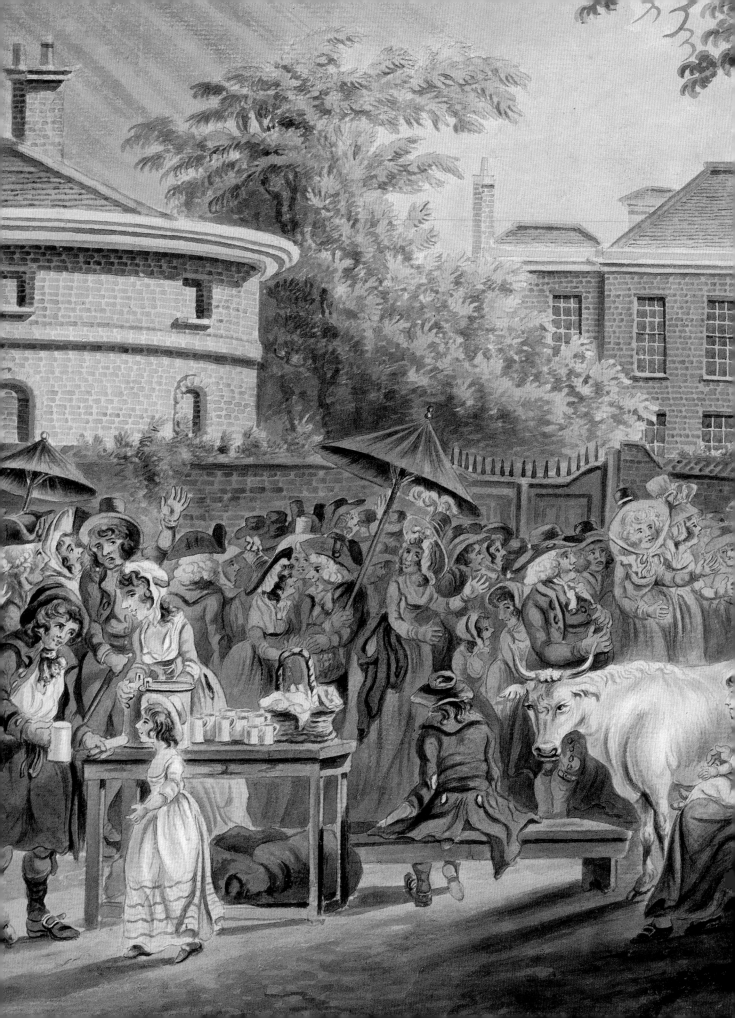

plain cold food, eaten informally in the spirit of a picnic, and a range of wines, table beer and cider.[35] In its heyday every one went there, from the Prince of Wales to common prostitutes. Vulgarity jostled with gentility apeing the *haut ton*.

Known by the end of the century as Vauxhall Gardens, its popularity earned it a place in literature. Writers from Goldsmith to Thackeray described the supper, which became a byword for its stingy portions, poor quality and high prices. Chickens the size of sparrows and almost transparent slices of ham and beef remained stock jokes until the gardens closed in 1859. Husbands irritatingly calculated Tyers' profits, while their wives and daughters did their best to enjoy their cheesecakes and custards.[36] However, most people were prepared to put up the mediocre fare just to be seen at one of London's most fashionable resorts.

The more exclusive Ranelagh Gardens in Chelsea offered very simple refreshments, which were included in the admission price of 2s 6d. An invitation to tender, issued in 1778, specifies the provision of 'the best hyson, or green tea; the best Turkey coffee, roasted fresh every day; the best Epping butter and milk; finest loaf sugar, and the fine rolls used at Ranelagh'.[37] The focus of the gardens was the Rotunda built in the style of the Pantheon in Rome. Inside an orchestra played while the company paraded round the central area, bowing and flirting and observing. Matthew Bramble found the spectacle absurd: 'One half of the company are following at the other's tails, in an eternal circle; like so many blind asses in an olive-mill…; while the other half are drinking hot water, under the denomination of tea, till nine or ten o'clock at night, to keep them awake for the rest of the evening.'[38]

Tea gardens offered similar pleasures on a more modest scale. Tea could be taken in the tearoom or in rustic arbours in the gardens, which were laid out with lawns, walks, ponds and statues. Outings to the suburban gardens were popular with the middle classes, particularly on Sundays. White Conduit House in Islington was a favoured destination for its wholesome air, fine views and rural situation. In 1754 its proprietor offered hot loaves, tea, coffee and liquors 'in the greatest perfection'. He assured his customers that the milk came straight from his cows, which were fed in open pasture, not on grain and confined in stalls as in the city.[39] Kentish Town and Holloway were also noted for the quality of their dairy herds and were popular resorts for those who liked syllabubs, cheesecakes and custards.

43. Milk could be bought straight from the cow in St James' Park and the Mall guaranteeing its purity. Most of the customers were children brought by their mothers and nursemaids (*The Mall with Carlton House Stables in the Background* by John Nixon, *c.*1785).

Focus   The Roast Beef of England Lucy Peltz

■

■

■

■

A letter to *The Connoisseur* in 1764 described the sensory pleasures of roast beef: 'juicy collops of fat and lean, that come swimming in gravy, and smoking most deliciously under our nostrils'.[40] Such a vivid account may well have titillated the reader's taste buds but, more importantly in the 18th century, it would also have encouraged their feelings of national pride. Known as the 'Roast Beef of Old England', a hearty slab of beef was the ultimate symbol of England's prosperity, especially as contrasted with the artificial sauces and scant salads of France.

Above left
44. George Smith of Chichester's oil painting *Still Life with Joint of Beef on a Pewter Dish* (c.1750–60) celebrates the simple, yet symbolic, national dish of roast beef as it would have been served in a tavern or inn.

Above right
45. Silver tankard with scroll handle, made by John Pero (c.1735–36), engraved with the arms and emblems of John Rich's Beefsteak Club, a jocular dining club whose patriotism was summed up in their motto 'Beef and Liberty'.

Diners readily identified the eating of beef, affectionately dubbed 'Sir Loin', as their national birthright and as evidence of their patriotism.[41] Steak, too, carried the same associations, and this is nowhere more evident than in the Sublime Society of Beefsteaks, founded in 1735 by John Rich, manager of Covent Garden Theatre. This society of artists and actors, which included William Hogarth among its corpus, met weekly to exchange witticisms, play practical jokes and otherwise indulge. Steak, ritually grilled at the fireplace, was the only meat they would allow, and this was celebrated in their insignia of a gridiron and their motto 'Beef and Liberty'.

Roast beef also played an important part in bolstering national confidence during times of war. Hogarth's famous *O the Roast Beef of Old England* (1748), set at Calais Gate shortly before the Peace of Aix-la-Chapelle, condemned the Catholic French and their Jacobite sympathies. Though a foppish French chef struggles under a haunch of beef, the proddings of a fat friar imply whose table this is destined for. By contrast, the two soldiers carrying a cauldron of watery *soupe maigre* allayed English fears of French

invasion by suggesting the malnutrition, low morale and general corruption of the enemy.

The French did not succeed in invading England, but the constant influx of French wines and cheeses and the English taste for their cuisine caused concern. In Louis-Phillipe Boitard's satire *The Imports of Great Britain from France* (1757) a group of 'high liv'd epicures' who cannot stomach honest English food disloyally await the arrival of their new French chef. Additionally, this engraving's dedication to the Society of Anti-Gallicans, a society of merchants and gentlemen who championed British goods over French competition, reminds us that during the 18th century the struggle with France was economic as well as military.

Many English people welcomed the start of the French revolution in 1789, but the growing violence provoked a return to anti-French satire. Once again, images of the difference between France and England, 'defined in terms of food', were central to the propagandist's armoury.[42] With the abolition of rank in France even former aristocrats were depicted as dishevelled and starving *sans-culottes*: in contrast, England's liberty was personified by John Bull who always came equipped with his smoking side of beef, his full belly and his beer.

Above left
46. Detail from William Hogarth's oil painting *O The Roast Beef of Old England* (1748) was painted during the armistice before the peace of Aix-la-Chapelle when anti-French feelings still ran high.

Above right
47. Published in the middle of the Seven Years War with France, Louis Phillipe Boitard's engraving *The Imports of Great Britain from France* (1757) criticised London's tastes for French cheeses, wines and cooking as unpatriotic, tantamount to opening England up to commercial invasion.

Left
48. Thomas Rowlandson's *French Liberty/British Slavery* (1792) shows the enduring power of a side of roast beef in the 18th century British immigration. A corpulent John Bull tucks into a copious supper while the French sans-culotte is imagined starving, despite his new-found 'liberty'.

19th century

Edwina Ehrman

Three major changes occurred in the 19th century that altered the experience of eating out in London. French *haute cuisine* became available to the public for the first time, restaurants created a new venue for eating out and the hotel was re-invented to provide an environment for entertaining outside the home. These changes laid the foundations for today's experience of eating in restaurants. Only a small percentage of Londoners enjoyed genuine French cooking or ate in restaurants during the 19th century, but chefs like Ude, Soyer, Francatelli and Escoffier became household names. Their cookery books demonstrated excitingly different ways of preparing and presenting food. By 1900 Londoners were more receptive to food than ever before and the way lay open for the explosion of eating styles that has been such a feature of the 20th century.

FOOD WRITING AND THE FIRST GOOD FOOD GUIDE

During the 19th century there is evidence of a greater public awareness of the possibilities of preparing food in new ways and in particular of the experience of eating outside the home. For the first time food became a subject worthy of serious study and intellectual discussion, and food writing became a separate genre; there was no longer a sense that the content needed to be morally validated. English food writers such as Abraham Hayward acknowledged their debt to the French pioneers, notably the *Almanach des Gourmands*, edited by Grimod de La Reynière, and *La Physiologie du goût* by Jean-Anthelme Brillat-Savarin.[1] Both Hayward and William Blanchard Jerrold cite Thomas Walker as the first British authority on gastronomy, and Hayward quotes extensively from his work, notably on the subject of whitebait dinners.[2] Jerrold claimed to be filling a gap in the market with his 1868 publication *The Epicure's Year Book and Table Companion*. It includes sections on topics such as 'The Seasons in the Kitchen', 'Remarkable Dinners of 1867', 'London Dinners', 'Good Living in Paris', 'Cooks and the Art of Cookery' and 'The Epicure's Library'.[3] Sadly, Jerrold's ambition of producing a yearbook failed, as had an earlier publication with similar aims, *The Epicure's Almanack, or Calendar of Good Living in London*. Published in 1815 and modelled on the *Almanach des Gourmands*, it was the first directory to London's inns, taverns, coffee-houses, eating-houses and other places of 'alimentary Resort'.[4]

49. *A-la-mode* beef was popular in the 19th-century and some eating houses made it a speciality (*The Advantages of Travel – or – 'A Little Learning is a Dangerous Thing'* by George Cruikshank, 1824).

50. Tavern sign for The Goose and Gridiron, St Paul's Churchyard. 'Here, if there is not always a goose ready for the gridiron, there is a gridiron ready for the goose, or any other bird or beast …. Here are also joints of all sorts, hot from one o'clock until five.' (*Epicure's Almanack*, 1815).

The Epicure's Almanack is a mine of information. It includes a wide-ranging guide to London's eating places, a survey of the markets, a seasonal calendar and a review of the principal tradesmen supplying the most up-to-date appliances and equipment for the kitchen and dining room. The criteria used for judging the eating establishments reflect many of today's standards. Dining rooms are praised for being well lit, spacious, tastefully fitted up and clean, and criticised for poor ventilation. Efficient, pleasant service and special personal qualities are noted. The author particularly commended the recent adoption by some houses of written bills of fare with fixed prices, which he saw as a huge improvement on the waiters' 'culinary oratory'.

The most striking development revealed by the guide is the number of eating places specialising in particular foods. Ham Shops and Ham and Beef Shops usually sold ham, beef and tongue by the plate or by weight, continental sausages, and sometimes soup, which was a popular fast food. Handsome scales dominated the shop windows, which were festooned with joints of meat. Evett's Ham Shop in Red Lion Passage also sold take-away ham sandwiches, wrapped in cabbage leaves to keep them fresh.[5] Garraway's Coffee House was also recommended for its ready-cut sandwiches. Trays of ham, beef and tongue were prepared for the lunch-time rush which started between 11 and 12 noon.[6] Oyster Warehouses, Oyster Rooms and Shellfish Shops sprang up, offering a take-away service as well as seating, imitating similar places at Billingsgate. The shops were partly open to the street and displayed barrels of oysters and shellfish on the counter.

Another 19th-century innovation was the A-la-Mode Beef Shop. Beef *à la mode* was a dish of beef and calves' feet slowly stewed with carrots and onions and flavoured with herbs. Crish's at 20 Butcher Lane was said to serve beef in every way, with the proper accompaniments of endive, red beetroot and French rolls. All the meat used by Mr Crish was fresh and fed on pasture – not from cattle kept in stalls or stables;[7] such a claim has a resonance today, with its concerns about the quality of food. Offering a speciality enabled these establishments to promote a clear identity, and limited menus enabled them to provide a fast-service alternative to the chop house. Throughout the century shop and office workers patronised dining rooms, coffee-houses and chop houses which offered modestly priced and swiftly prepared meals at midday and before they travelled home to the suburbs.[8]

FRENCH COOKING AND CLUB DINING

French or French-style cooking had been available in London since the Restoration. However, following the break-up of the aristocratic French households during the Revolution, many more cooks and chefs travelled to England. Among them was Louis Eustache Ude, who had been employed in the kitchens of Louis XVI. After working for the Duke of Sefton for over twenty years he became steward to the United Service Club and worked for the Duke of York before being appointed to Crockford's in 1828. Crockford's was London's most fashionable and elite gambling club which, under Ude's direction, immediately gained a reputation for first-class cuisine. Accounts and memoirs of the time describe Ude with many of the characteristics we now associate with celebrity chefs. He was arrogant and supremely confident of his own talent; he could be confrontational and bad tempered, loved gossip and scandal and enjoyed a reputation as a wit. He was paid the astonishingly high salary of 1,000 guineas[9] a year and is said to have resigned when the committee refused to almost quadruple it. On the other hand his portrait by Daniel Maclise in *Fraser's Magazine* in 1832 shows him in a more contemplative mood, clasping a ladle and ruminating on his art.

AUTHOR OF "THE FRENCH COOK".

51. Louis Eustache Ude by Daniel Maclise. Before working at Crockford's Ude was employed as chef by the Duke of York. When he died, Ude quipped: 'Ah, mon pauvre Duc! How much will you miss me where you are gone!' (*Fraser's Magazine*, June 1832).

Ude and other French chefs such as M. Jacquier at the Clarendon Hotel, which according to the socialite Captain Gronow was 'the only hotel where you could get a genuine French dinner', enabled a small section of London society to eat good French food outside the homes of the very rich. To eat at the Clarendon was undeniably expensive: dinner cost £3 to £4 and a bottle of champagne or claret a guinea in 1814.[10]

Chefs like Ude also introduced French discipline to English kitchens. In *The French Cook; or, The Art of Cookery* Ude describes the qualities he felt were essential to a successful cook.[11] He should be intelligent, sober, industrious, and prepared to spend long hours practising and refining his cooking. His dishes must please the eye but he must balance creativity with practicality and economy; he must be able to manage time and staff and run his kitchen in a hygienic way. Above all, he must remember that the customer comes first and that his wishes must be met without a murmur of complaint.

The July Revolution that toppled Charles X of France in 1830 brought another French cook to England. Alexis Soyer arrived in London with the recommendation of having been head chef at La Maison Douix, a fashionable Paris restaurant. After working in private households, he was appointed the first *chef de cuisine* at the recently established Reform Club in Pall Mall. The Reform was set up by a group of Whigs and Radicals to promote parliamentary reform and had about 1,250 members when it opened in 1836.

When Soyer joined the staff in 1837 plans were under way to expand and rebuild the clubhouse and kitchens to designs by Charles Barry. Soyer's finished kitchen reveals his systematic approach, his appreciation of the latest technology and his inventiveness. Its layout linked the different departments in the most logical and space-efficient way. Gas, a new medium for cooking, was introduced in the principal kitchen. Soyer praised its efficiency and flexibility in a detailed article written for *The Builder*.[12] Steam was used for cooking and to warm heated cupboards for plates and prepared food. Soyer was particularly pleased with the design of the ice drawers, which were fitted with drains to carry away the ice water to a waste pipe, so saving labour and time. The kitchen attracted many visitors and Soyer enjoyed giving the more eminent a guided tour. Jerrold praised clubs for creating a generation of educated eaters who would demand better standards: 'If the princely kitchens have

decayed, the number of people who know how to eat has vastly increased. Clubs have spread among men of modest fortune a knowledge of refined cookery'.[13]

In *The Gastronomic Regenerator*[14] Soyer boasted that in the ten months it had taken him to write the cookery book he had provided 25,000 dinners for members of the club, daily meals for 60 servants, had prepared 38 special dinners and had welcomed 15,000 visitors to the kitchen. The Coffee Room Complaints Books kept by the club give some idea of the food favoured by the members and of problems in the kitchen. Typical complaints include 'beef tough, potatoes cold', 'omelette bad and no oysters', 'the veal not good and badly dressed' and 'the fish very indifferent'. Members also grumbled about the price of food. The committee swiftly countered these complaints by quoting market prices and pointing out the small margins charged by the club. In response to a complaint from M.D. Gillow[15] it pointed out that the fowl for which he had been charged 4s 6d cost 4s at market but, as in other cases, conceded that in future prawns would be charged at cost. Writers of the period point out how well priced club meals were in comparison with similar meals in London.[16]

The simple fare routinely eaten in the coffee room was hardly a test of Soyer's skills, but the special dinners held at the club allowed his culinary imagination to soar. One of the most famous was the banquet held on 3 July 1846 in honour of Ibrahim Pacha, the Ottoman general. A full account, including the menu, was published in

52. This sectional view of the Reform Club kitchen shows all the elements of the kitchen department, including the larders and scullery. Soyer had his own spacious office to the left of the principal kitchen (*The Kitchen Department at the Reform Club* by John Tarring, 1842).

The Illustrated London News.[17] Among the *relèves de rôts*, which formed the finale to the dinner, was a dessert made in honour of the Pacha called *La Crème d'Egypte, à l'Ibrahim Pacha.* Shaped in the form of the base of a pyramid made from light meringue cake and surrounded with fruit, it supported a *crème à l'ananas* on the top of which was placed a portrait of the general's father, Mehemet Ali. Soyer's cooking and *The Gastronomic Regenerator* were lavishly praised by his contemporaries: 'Mr Soyer's Regenerator is indeed a work of merit…. It enhances the value of the chef de cuisine of the Reform Club and has introduced quite a reform in the Art of Cookery, Poor Ude is dead, Carême also, Soyer lives, need I say more'.[18] Jerrold, however, described Soyer's 'Hundred Guinea' dishes as 'vulgarities' and did not consider him in the same league as chefs like Ude and Francatelli, who succeeded Ude at Crockford's and later worked at the Reform. Perhaps Thackeray, who caricatured Soyer as M. Alcide Mirobolant in his novel *Pendennis* (1848) should have the last word. He recommended simplicity and temperance in eating: '…beef steak, if you are hungry, [is] as good as turtle; bottled ale, if you like it, to the full good as champagne; there is no delicacy in the world which Monsieur Francatelli or Monsieur Soyer can produce which I believe to be better than toasted cheese…'.[19] 18th-century tastes lived on.

SOUP KITCHENS, COOKSHOPS AND COFFEE-SHOPS

Soyer published other cookery books including *The Modern Housewife* (1849), a best-seller written for the middle-class market, and *Soyer's Shilling Cookery for the People* (1854), written for 'artisans, mechanics and cottagers'. His experience of working with the poor resulted in a pamphlet with recipes for soup.[20] It cost 6d, and 1d from each copy sold went to charity. Soyer had been shocked by the hardship suffered by the poor in 1845–46 when meagre corn harvests, which affected the price and availability of bread, coincided with the failure of the Irish potato crop. In addition, the economy was depressed and industries were failing. On 10 February 1847 he wrote to *The Times* with a proposal to set up a model soup kitchen, personally donating £30 towards the project. He was particularly concerned about the quality of soup and in a subsequent letter included two recipes The main ingredients were beef, vegetables, pearl barley or rice, flour and water. A hundred gallons cost £1. The vegetables peelings, green part of the leeks and leaves of celery were all to be used for, as he explained: 'it is a well known fact, that the exterior of every vegetable, roots in particular, contains more flavour than the interior of it'.[21] It is not clear if he understood the nutritional value of his recommendation.

At the government's request Soyer set up his first soup kitchen in Dublin. Each person received a quart (1,100ml) of soup and ¼lb of bread or a savoury biscuit. One thousand people an hour could be fed. Those too ill or infirm to visit the kitchen had soup brought to their homes in a heated cart. Back in London, Soyer continued to raise public awareness of the conditions of the poor and set up his next kitchen in Spitalfields, where the weaving industry was in decline, unemployment high and many families destitute. A choice of beef soup, peas panada or rice curry was offered

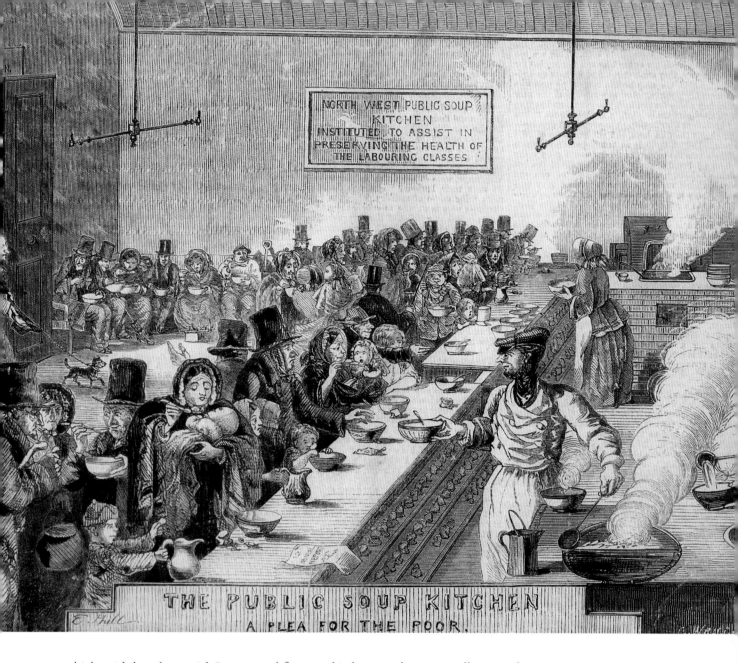

which, with bread, cost 1d. It was usual for soup kitchens to charge a small sum and to sell tickets for free meals to charitable members of the public to distribute to the poor of their choice. The North-West Public Soup Kitchen operated this system but charged 2 ½d for either a quart of beef or pea soup or 2lbs of rice milk with a roll of bread.[22]

These charitable initiatives and many others relied on fund raising for their support and then, as now, meals played an important part. 'English charity, gracious and ever-ready, yet carries a knife and fork in the folds of her garments. Heady port loosens the purse strings in the City. In the West, the dinner that flatters the diner lands the subscription'.[23] In the city, the Albion, the London and Freemasons' Tavern were popular venues for public dinners. George Augustus Sala ridiculed the practice in his fictional account of a fund-raising dinner for the Asylum of Fatuous Monomaniacs, pointing out that the cost of the meal alone would provide huge benefit to the needy.[24] However, he admitted that the system worked.

53. The North-West Public Soup Kitchen was set up in 1846 at 295 Euston Road. It served beef soup made from ox head, pea soup and rice milk. In cold weather as much as 140 gallons of soup were distributed to about 550 people everyday (*The Illustrated Times*, 18 December 1858).

54. This plate made by Davenport was part of a service used around 1830 at the London Tavern, famous for civic and charitable dinners. Its cellars contained an excellent stock of wine and tanks for the turtles destined to appear on its tables.

The poor continued to be dependent on the services of the neighbourhood cookshop, tripe shop and modest eating-house. The best of these establishments offered basic food at a reasonable price in ordered but cramped surroundings. In the most deprived areas like St Giles cookshops remained noisome but the food they offered had changed: '… little dens, reeking of the odours of fried fish, sausages, and baked potatoes, or steaming with reminders of *à la mode* beef and hot eel soup, offer suppers, cheap and nasty, to the poor in pocket'.[25] Fried fish and baked potatoes were both new cheap convenience foods in the Victorian period. Stale fish could be bought cheaply and frying arrested its deterioration. The eating-houses selling fish and potatoes were the antecedents of fish and chip shops. George Gissing described one in Whitecross Street in his 1880 novel *Workers in the Dawn*:

'Behind the long counter stands a man and a woman, the former busy in frying flat fish over a huge fire, the latter engaged in dipping a ladle into a large vessel which steams profusely; and in front of the counter stands a row of hungry-looking people, devouring eagerly the flakes of fish and greasy potatoes as they come from the pan, whilst others are served by the woman to little basins of stewed eels from the steaming tureen.'[26]

Skilled workers often ate in coffee shops, which George Dodd described as 'one of the creations of modern London society'.[27] Import duties on coffee were lowered in 1808 and halved in 1825, making it an affordable alternative to alcohol for working people. The first shops were set up after the 1808 reduction and by 1840 there were 1,800. They served hot drinks and non-alcoholic beverages like ginger beer, and offered breakfast, simple dinners and coffee in the evenings. The provision of newspapers and periodicals attracted the respectable artisan who was keen to better himself. Francis Place felt that they were 'the means of great improvement to working people'[28], and Dodd concurred: 'there can be little question that these places conduce to sobriety and general intelligence'.

ADULTERATION

Coffee was one of the foods examined by Dr Arthur Hassall in his wide-ranging report on the methods and extent of food adulteration, commissioned by *The Lancet* in 1850. He found it was almost invariably mixed with chicory and other substances such as mangel-wurzel, acorn and red oxide of lead, which was used to colour the chicory. Bread was adulterated with alum, which whitened inferior grades of flour and the flour itself often mixed with potatoes, peas, beans, gypsum and chalk. Pickles, bottled vegetables and fruit were cooked in copper pans to make them green and fresh looking, and other poisons were used to colour preserved meat and fish. Hassall's conclusion was that adulteration was widespread and deep rooted. Importantly his report also named and shamed those found guilty of adulteration.

Concerns over adulterations were nothing new. Smollett, in the persona of Matthew Bramble, in *The Expedition of Humphry Clinker* complained in 1771: 'The bread I eat in London, is a deleterious paste, mixed up with chalk, alum and bone ashes; insipid to the taste and destructive to the constitution'.[29]

Other investigations confirmed *The Lancet's* findings. Initially the government was reluctant to intervene in accordance with its belief that the economy was best governed by supply and demand supported by free competition. However, despite some efforts by the up-market sector of the food industry at self-reformation, it was persuaded to act by force of public opinion. This resulted in several acts culminating in the 1875 Sale of Food and Drugs Act, which is the basis of the present law. Inspectors and public analysts were appointed and adulteration clearly defined. It brought about a huge improvement in standards and, by the 1880s, the quality of basic food and drink, like bread, tea and beer, was rarely found to be at fault.[30]

ETHNIC FOOD

Immigrants to London naturally went to live in areas of the city where their countrymen were already established, where they could make useful contacts, speak their own language and eat familiar food. Many Italians settled in Holborn and Clerkenwell, others lived in Soho: 'This neighbourhood is savoury with macaroni and oils, betokening the presence of the Italian element who flock to Soho Square in great numbers when they arrive in London. There are 'albergos' and wine shops where you may obtain a quarter of a fowl for 9d, and a bottle of marsala, and you can get olives and brandied cherries, at desert, for a few pence'.

Women waited at tables serving organ grinders, plaster figure sellers, musicians and porters working in Italian warehouses, medical students, hack journalists and writers.[31] There was also a long-established French community in Soho and around Leicester Square. The whole area had something of the atmosphere of a continental town. The air was scented with tobacco and garlic, foreign newspapers were available, and French, Spanish, Italians, Poles, Greeks and Germans mingled in shabby café-restaurants playing cards and dominoes. Jerrold recommended the eating-houses in Soho and the delicatessens and market and contrasted the 'luxurious' foods with the

55. The sign recording the partnership of Battista Bolla and Carlo Gatti in 1849 can still be seen in this late 19th-century view. Both men came from the canton of Ticino in Switzerland. Gatti rapidly built up an extensive business in the ice and restaurant trade (*View of Ridler's Hotel and Bolla's Restaurant in Holborn Hill* by T.G. Fraser, *c.*1890).

squalid conditions in which the immigrants lived.[32] Many French, Italian and Swiss immigrants worked in the catering business as café and restaurant owners, confectioners and *chocolatiers*, cooks, waiters and service staff.

The Jewish community living to the east of the city had their own shops and markets selling kosher food. Market stalls in Duke's Place sold hot hard-boiled eggs and hot peas and lentils. Many shops in the area sold fried fish, a Jewish speciality recommended by several cookery writers. Ann Battam, who published 'a collection of some very scarce and valuable receipts' in 1750, included a recipe for 'The Jews Way of Frying Fish' as did Soyer in *The Gastronomic Regenerator* almost 100 years later.

Despite Britain's long-established links with India[33] there was only one short-lived Indian-run eating place in London in the 19th century. The first published Indian-style recipes appeared in Hannah Glasse's cookery book in 1747.[34] When, in 1811, Dean Mahomet advertised his Hindostanee Coffee-House at 34 George Street, Portman Square, he promised 'Indian dishes, in the highest perfection, and allowed by epicures to be unequalled to any curries ever made in England'.[35] Dean Mahomet was a subaltern in the English army in India before following his patron and commander to Ireland in 1784. He established himself in Cork, married and published his *Travels* but in 1807 decided to move to London.[36] The coffee-house, which opened in 1809, is described in *The Epicure's Almanack*. It was furnished with bamboo chairs and sofas and decorated with 'Chinese pictures and other Asiatic embellishments'. A hookah for smoking Chilm tobacco was provided. 'All the dishes were dressed with Curry-powder, rice, Cayenne and the best spices of Arabia'.[37] Initially successful the coffee-house ran into problems, and Dean Mahomet petitioned for bankruptcy in 1812.

Another venue providing a home from home for 'Indian gentlemen' was the Oriental Club, established in 1824. In 1861 Richard Terry, the *chef de cuisine*, published a collection of recipes 'gathered not only from my own knowledge of Cookery, but from Native Cooks...'.[38] By the middle of the century the use of curry was well established in English cooking. The catalogue[39] for the sale of Vauxhall Gardens in 1859 included five jars of curry powder and two of curry 'pest', and soup kitchens offered curried rice. The first restaurant known to employ an Indian cook in the 19th century was the Savoy, which served Indian, Russian and German dishes alongside English cooking and French cuisine.

The Savoy also included American dishes in its menus: '... a marked importance will be given to the special products of the United States – canvas-back ducks, terrapin, clams, American oysters, green corn and other luxuries being imported as in season, so that travelling Americans will be well catered for'.[40] From the late 1860s grill rooms had been set up in London restaurants and hotels and American bars soon followed. In 1885 'Bacchus' published a handbook[41] 'for the management of Hotel and American Bars, and the Manufacture of the New and Fashionable drinks'. It includes recipes for a range of cocktails and advice on how to arrange the bar.

THE RESTAURANT AND HOTEL DINING

A significant development of the 19th century was the arrival of the restaurant and modern hotel, which both provided acceptable public surroundings for mixed dining. In 1851 the influx of visitors to London to see the Great Exhibition focused attention on the shortage of suitable venues for men and women eating together. Women could eat alone at confectioners' shops, as they had done since the beginning of the century[42], and in 'Parisian cafés' at the fashionable Thames-side resorts such as Windsor, Richmond and Greenwich. In London, café-restaurants like Epitaux's in Pall Mall and Verey's in Regent Street were both considered suitable.[43] Jane Welch Carlyle wrote to her husband in 1852 about her visits to Verey's, where she had a 'beautiful little mutton chop and glass of bitter ale!... The *chaarge* at Verey's is very moderate, and the cooking *perfect*. For my dinner and ale today I paid one and fivepence...for the outrage to '*delicate femaleism*', I am beyond all such considerations at present. However I see single women beside myself at Verey's – not improper – governesses and the like.'[44]

More conventional or less confident women could eat in the separate ladies' dining rooms provided by some establishments. At the end of the century the cafés and refreshment rooms introduced in shops and department stores like Liberty and Whiteley's offered another alternative for women up in town. However, for families or mixed parties there were few places where a meal could be eaten. 'It is true that, since our intercourse with the Continent, some coffee-houses have been opened where

MANNERS · AND · CVSTOMS · OF · Yᵈ · ENGLYSHE · IN · 1849 · ·. Nº · 26 ·

BLACKWALL · SHOWYNGE · Yᵈ · PVBLICK · A · DINYNGE · ON · WRYTEBAIT ·

56. Although whitebait dinners at Greenwich and Blackwall are usually represented as a masculine opportunity for over-indulgence, women enjoyed them too. This cartoon shows Lovegrove's Tavern at Blackwall, which had a fine view over the Thames (from *Manners and Customs of ye Englyshe* by Richard Doyle, 1849).

gentlemen may take their wives and daughters; but it is not yet become a recognised custom…'.[45] Increasing middle-class demands for respectable eating places, suitable for members of both sexes, undoubtedly encouraged the growth of restaurants.

London restaurants were modelled on the continental type and many were established or run by French and Swiss Italians. An early use of the term 'restaurateur' is found in *The Epicure's Alamanack* (1815) describing the proprietors of three eating places in the vicinity of Leicester Square, all of whom have French surnames.[46] One was said to offer 'an excellent dinner cooked in the French manner, at a very small charge' while the others offered English cooking and continental styles. However, by the 1850s some proprietors were adopting the term 'restaurant' to distance themselves from the traditional dining rooms, which were associated with business and trade, and to reposition themselves in the most fashionable sector of the market. Simpson's Grand Restauratum[47], established in 1848 in the Strand, led the way in creating a light and spacious dining room furnished with tables as well as boxes. Its retention of boxes shows it to have been a transitional layout, but it had more of the ambience of a restaurant or club dining room than a chop house. Some City dining rooms also re-branded themselves as restaurants. Sala dismissed them as 'pseudo "restaurants" '; ' … they give you things with French names, charge you a stated sum for attendance, provide the pale ale in silver tankards, and take care of your hat and coat; but I like them not…'[48] These 'restaurants' offered separate ladies' dining rooms, rather than facilities for mixed dining.

However the café-restaurants run by French and Swiss-Italian entrepreneurs were increasingly patronised by couples. They were decorated in continental style with plate glass mirrors, red plush and lavish gilding but the cuisine, as at Gatti's in the Strand, was usually English or Anglo-French. One of the most successful was the Café Royal founded in 1865 by Daniel Nicolas Thévenon. It was famous for its bohemian clientele, which included *fin de siècle* personalities like James McNeil Whistler, Aubrey Beardsley and Oscar Wilde, who held court in the Domino Room. Its restaurant offered a dinner 'absoluement comme à Paris' with wines to match.[49] Bookings could be made by telegraph to 'Restaurant London' or from 1897 by telephone. Italian food could be eaten at Pagani's in Great Portland Street, Pinoli's in the Strand, Torrino's in Oxford Street and Previtali's in Leicester Square and German food at the Café de Paris on Ludgate Hill.

During the 1860s the catering industry became more commercialised and partnerships and limited companies were set up to build and run restaurants and hotels. Between 1866 and 1874, 116 companies involved in the hotel and restaurant trade were registered.[50]

In 1868 Frederick Gordon, a leading entrepreneur, leased Crosby Hall, a 15th-century building in Bishopsgate, to convert it into a restaurant. The dining room was open to men and women, and waitresses, not waiters, attended the tables. The provision of a ladies' 'boudoir' and retiring rooms with female attendants shows that Gordon was actively seeking women customers.[51]

The Criterion Restaurant and Theatre built by Spiers and Pond and designed by Thomas Verity opened in 1874. Its spacious and varied accommodation, opulent interiors and comfortable carpeted dining areas with flowers on the tables set a benchmark for future developments. Dinners were served at a range of prices with more costly but good French cuisine offered in the fashionable 'East Rooms'. Supper was available before and after the theatre. By the 1880s it was quite acceptable for women to eat in male company in respectable restaurants in 'good' areas.[52] Soho was still too bohemian, and the Haymarket with its oyster bars, 'night houses' and swarms of prostitutes shockingly louche.

The first companies to build hotels were the railway companies, which enhanced their service, and increased their profits, by providing accommodation and refreshments at their London termini. Until the 1830s travellers had the choice of staying at inns, taverns, coffee-houses or family-run hotels, converted from domestic housing. The London and Birmingham railway were the first to form a syndicate, to build two hotels, which opened at Euston Station in 1839. As new networks developed, all the companies with a London terminus, except the London & South Western Railway, built hotels. St Pancras station and its hotel, the Midland Grand, were built at the height of the railway construction era to designs by Sir George Gilbert Scott. The high Gothic style of the exterior was carried through into the hotel, which

57. The London Bridge Railway Terminus Hotel opened in 1862. This was the principal coffee room. A smaller one, decorated in the same style, was available for the use of ladies only (*The London Bridge Terminus Coffee Room* by Robert Dudley, *c.*1862).

opened in 1873. The magnificent 100-ft long coffee-room, which followed the curved line of the west wing, was embellished with painted ironwork, a coffered ceiling and a decorative frieze above the entablature. The first manager was Robert Etzensberger, from the Victoria Hotel in Venice. Under his supervision the coffee-room was equipped with plate from Elkingtons, china from the Royal Porcelain Company in Worcester and glass from P. & C. Osler. Gillow made the furniture, including four easy chairs for the coffee-room designed by Scott. A ladies' dining room and reading room graced the first floor. The cellar included wines from Austria, Hungary and the Levant and in 1879 its *table d'hôte* dinner at 5s was the only railway hotel meal to be commended in *Dickens's Dictionary of London*.[53]

Following the success of the railway hotels other companies built hotels across the capital. The first was the Westminster Palace Hotel in 1860. This was followed by the Langham, in Portland Place, which opened in 1865. Unlike the traditional family-run hotels whose coffee rooms were restricted to men, their dining rooms were open to both sexes. The new hotels tried to emulate the standards set by hotels in Paris and New York: 'In conducting this establishment, an attempt has been made to introduce the best points of the three systems, English, French and American; the comfort of the first being amalgamated with the elegance of the second and the discipline and organisation of the third'.[54] American travellers were an important market in London and hotels competed for their custom.

The Savoy hotel, which was the brainchild of the impresario Richard D'Oyly Carte, was particularly designed to appeal to Americans. Not only did he provide his guests with electric light, elevators and more bathrooms than had ever been installed in a London hotel before but he also offered a selection of American dishes in the restaurant.[55] The hotel opened in 1889 with William Hardwick as the general manager and Monsieur Charpentier as chef.

Shortly before the opening a 'house-warming' party had been given for the hotel at a private dinner hosted by Mr and Mrs Hwfa Williams. Their guests included the well-connected, rich and fashionable, the menu was extravagant and the only wine served was Deutz and Geldermann Gold Lack '80. The party set the tone for the future and introduced a fashionable new place to entertain and dine out. *Diana's Diary* for 1 November 1890 describes an intimate dinner in the restaurant:

'Bob and I and a couple of congenial souls dined there, and we had one of the best cooked dinners we have had since we left Paris…Conversation during the repast never flagged, for it was all about food. (Mem. – Am beginning to think that the most brilliant of dinner talk is about food. So appropriate and a dissertation on each dish increases the enjoyment of it).'[56]

In January 1890 Cézar Ritz had joined the hotel as a general manager after lengthy negotiations with D'Oyly Carte, and in July Auguste Escoffier came as chef. Ritz and Escoffier were a potent combination and the meals and service at the hotel became legendary.

By the close of the century the patterns of eating familiar to us today were in place. Mealtimes had altered to suit changing lifestyles, and more emphasis was placed on the evening meal. In affluent households breakfast was followed after midday by luncheon, with dinner sometimes as late as 8.30 pm or 9.00 pm by the end of the century. Afternoon tea filled the gap between lunch and dinner. Restaurants responded to these changes by offering a later service and appropriate menus. Another change was the replacement of the *service à la Française* by the *service à la Russe*, introduced by the aristocracy in the 1820s,[57] where waiters served each course according to current practice. Food came to the table hotter and guests no longer had to serve each other. But diners could not pick and choose as they had in the past, and the constant presence of waiters could be intrusive.

Focus

Street Food–Welks and Penny Licks Edwina Ehrman

■

■

■

■

'Whelks were heaped in thousands on the heads of barrels and tables, and ham sandwiches at a penny a piece, and boiled potatoes with sheep's trotters, oysters, fried fish and every kind of fruit and vegetable were for sale.'

So wrote Daniel Kirwan, the London correspondent of *The New York World*, in 1870 about the Saturday evening market at New Cut in Lambeth. Fast-food sellers did a brisk trade at Saturday markets, thronged with working people who had just received their wages. Twenty years earlier Henry Mayhew, also a journalist, had co-ordinated an

exhaustive survey of London's street sellers. He argued that the most important change to street food in the 19th century was the number of new foods for sale – baked potatoes, ham sandwiches, slices of pineapple, ice cream and ginger beer.

The coffee stall was another 19th-century innovation made viable by the fall in duty on coffee. In 1850 there were over 300. For some street sellers a simple barrow or makeshift stand was no longer sufficient. Mayhew described an exceptionally fine-wheeled coffee stall, painted bright green with an oilcloth awning and lit by brass-mounted oil lamps. It had four coffee urns and sold bread, butter, sandwiches and cake. Ginger beer fountains were introduced in about 1845. Hired from the manufacturers, they pumped air into the beer making it frothy so that the glasses appeared deceptively full. Potatoes were very popular, and portable potato cans, which kept the pre-cooked potatoes hot, could also be hired, or bought outright. Can owners took pride in their appearance, and some were highly polished and embellished with brass mounts.

The number of street sellers decreased throughout the century. Many traditional street foods were now sold from shops, which could afford to cut their margins by

Above left
58. Roast apple sellers were a rarity in the mid-19th century, displaced by changing tastes and the introduction of new hot foods like baked potatoes. (*Hot Codlins Seller* by Charles Cooper Henderson, *c*.1828).

Above right
59. Coffee stalls on the main roads were used by people going to work. The coffee was drunk from mugs or bowls, which were rinsed out in a tub kept under the stall (*Coffee Stall – Early Morning* by H. Pisan, after Gustave Doré, 1872).

maintaining a high turnover. By 1850 the hot pie men had lost nearly all their trade to pie shops, which offered larger penny pies than they could afford to sell. Eel, pie and mash shops took trade away from the hot eel sellers. In 1874 thirty-three eel and pie shops are listed in *Kelly's Trade Directory for London*.

Street sellers also lost business through the closure of traditional venues. Bartholomew Fair, held at Smithfield for three days in late August, was famous for its food. Hot sausages were cooked over glowing charcoal fires. Pie men and gingerbread merchants mingled with the crowd between stalls of fruit, sweets and pastries. The fair was abolished in 1855 after being part of London life for seven centuries.

Ice cream became increasingly popular. According to Mayhew, ice cream sellers were a rarity in 1850. Working people had had no experience of ices and suffered toothache by biting deeply into them. By the 1880s Italian controlled the market, making the ice cream at their homes in Clerkenwell. In 1900 there were about 900 ice cream barrows based in the district offering 1d and ½d 'licks' to an enthusiastic public.

Above left

60. A baked potato with salt and a slice of Irish butter cost 1d (detail from Barclay and Perkins' Brewery in Southwark, British School, 1835–40).

Above right

61. Ice cream was enormously popular with children. It was served in small glasses with a conical bowl called 'licks' (Halfpenny Ices by John Thomson from *Street Life in London*, 1877).

Left

62. This wheeled stand, which sold coffee, tea and ginger beer, as well as ham, beef and bread, was seen by the artist near Piccadilly between 1820 and 1830 (*W. Smith's Royal Stand* by George Scharf).

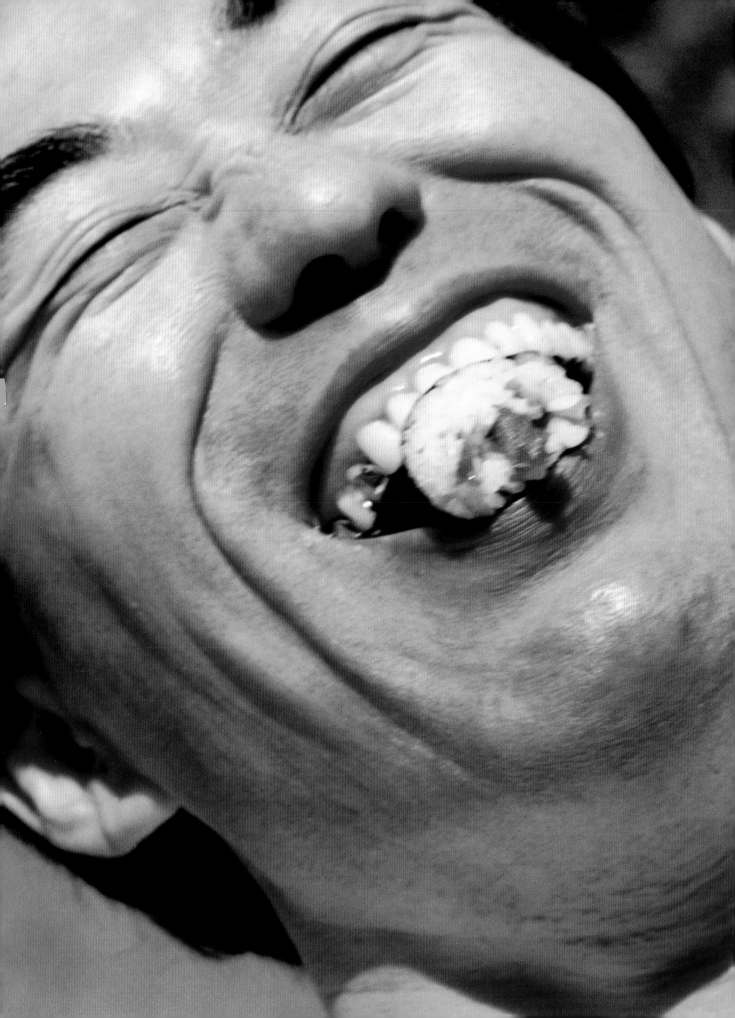

20th century

Cathy Ross

Eating out in London during the 20th century can be seen as the maturing of trends that began in the 19th. However change was on a more spectacular scale. London ends the 20th century with the title 'Restaurant capital of the world', a city where eating out is the social norm for most 7 million Londoners, all of whom, statistically, spend an average of £700 a year[1] in the pursuit of pleasure through the productions of professional cooks.

Many social and economic ingredients have combined to create this historically unprecedented situation, and three areas of change in particular are notable. The first is the spread of the eating-out habit to all sectors of society. Today few Londoners would consider a family outing to McDonald's an extraordinary event. One hundred years ago great swathes of London's working class population would have found the idea of eating out for fun inconceivable. As with many such leisure activities, the spread of pleasure eating was partly driven by increased affluence and partly by the opportunism of restaurateurs and caterers, who by the 20th century included not just ambitious individuals but also aggressive corporations.

The second change is in the type of meals consumed by Londoners when they ate out. Generally all meals got shorter and lighter as the century progressed, a trend sometimes attributed to women, whose ideal meal was said to be 'next to nothing, pleasantly served',[2] and sometimes to the young, 'who seem to live wholly on nibbles of *hors d'oeuvres*'.[3] Supper began to replace dinner, but the meal that assumed a new importance was lunch as the growth of London's modern transport system enabled workers to live at a distance from their place of work, thus eroding the traditional working man's habit of returning home for a midday meal. Astute caterers were quick to provide for the needs of the new commuting workforce, which now included women, and a whole range of new daytime eating institutions duly appeared, designed for lunch.

The final area of change is the food itself, more particularly the unprecedented expansion of choice in foods and cuisines available to the Londoner through the city's restaurants. Before World War One, London's West End offered only a few German restaurants, and one Chinese and one Indian as alternatives to the Italian, French and American cuisines that then dominated. By World War Two these had been joined by

63. A 20th-century Londoner eating out, 1999. Photograph by Torla Evans.

Greek, Turkish, Palestinian, Jewish, Russian, Spanish, Japanese, Brazilian, Hungarian and Egyptian restaurants.[4] Today London's gastronomic network encompasses the globe, and the city has also provided fertile ground for the new supra-national hybrid cuisines, 'Pacific rim', 'fusion' and of course 'new British'. It is a far cry from the beginning of the century when the author of a promotional booklet for the newly opened Trocadero restaurant wrote of his heartfelt relief at the prospect of escaping from old British cuisine: 'no more hunks of food flung at you as if you were a dog waiting to be fed, no more eternal round of British fare – heavy, solid, indigestible, and, for the most part badly cooked; no more gargantuan tankards of heady beer, or beakers, or rummers of punch, or British brandy; no more such abominations as English salad, namely, long lettuces, chopped fine and swimming in an abomination known as 'salad dressing' in a crinkled bottle; no more horrible British melted butter, or, as I call it 'paste sauce' that makes me shudder at the thought of it.'[5]

THE RESTAURANT AND EVENING EATING

As we saw in the last chapter, 'the restaurant' arrived in the 19th century. By the early 20th century it had developed an invasive vigour, which transformed the city, as Thomas Burke noted in 1934: 'Few people, I imagine, of the 1880s can have foreseen the enormous growth of [the restaurant] industry over the whole face of London. It scores next to transport as one of the visible factors of change in the life and habits of the people. To young people of today, a London without popular restaurants to which almost anyone can go for any sort of meal is almost inconceivable; yet fifty years ago it had very few, if any of that sort.'[6]

Why did this continental institution prove so irresistible to the English around the turn of the century? The simple explanation is that 'the restaurant dinner' became fashionable. According to a guidebook of 1908, 'Recent years have witnessed a remarkable change in the habits of London society and public restaurants are used for many dinner and supper parties that would formerly have been given at home'.[7] Six years earlier this remarkable change was clearly visible to Robert Machray: 'These restaurant dinners are comparatively recent institutions, so to speak, having come into

64. 'A Two-Penny Pie', 'The Restaurant Dinner', 'Dinner at the Café Boulogne, Soho'. Three illustrations by Tom Browne (1872–1910) for *The Night Side of London* by Robert Machray (1902).

vogue during the last few years, but they have become almost, if not altogether, the greatest feature of the Night Side of London high life'.[8]

The upper-class restaurant dinner could mimic the domestic dinner party in that a private room could be hired, and the hostess could discuss menus beforehand with her chosen restaurant chef. However, it still represented a fundamental shift of sociable eating from private to public. If fashion was the 'pull factor' in this shift, the 'push factor' was the shrinking number of servants in upper- and middle-class households, a trend emphasised by the growing popularity of mansion flats. Seen as a rather nasty innovation in the 1880s, the service flat with its small kitchen was a familiar part of London life by the 1930s.

Another element in the restaurant's new found fashionability was its association with all things bohemian and artistic, a perfect match for the fin-de-siècle frame of mind. Soho and the area north of Oxford Street later known as Fitzrovia were the key areas here, both meeting all the requirements of those seeking a romantic bohemian life – notably small, continental restaurants frequented by artists, philosophers and poets. The attraction of restaurants such as the Café Boulogne, Beguinot's and Schmidt's in Charlotte Street was not just their bohemian ambience but also their remarkably cheap meals; a table d'hôte dinner costing as little as 1s. The Soho shilling dinner became legendary: a 'Homeric bob's worth of hors-d'oeuvre, soup, omelette, chicken, cheese and coffee'.[9]

The association between bohemian restaurants and artists was most striking at La Tour Eiffel in Percy Street, established in 1908 by the Austrian chef Rudolph Stulik to

65. This group portrait of the Vorticists meeting at the Restaurant de la Tour Eiffel in Spring 1915 was painted from memory in the 1960s by William Roberts (1895–1980). Included in the group are the restaurant's waiter, Joe and, on the right, the chef-patron, Rudolph Stulik, holding one of his specialities, Gâteau St Honoré.

66. Design for the interior of Fischer's Restaurant in Bond Street by Raymond McGrath (1903–77), 1932.

become the meeting place for Imagist poets, Vorticist painters and other members of London's creative avant-garde.[10] In 1915 Stulik commissioned Wyndham Lewis to decorate one of the private dining rooms: the resulting 'Vorticist Room', famous in its day, has sadly not survived and nor have the mural panels painted in 1912 for Au Petit Savoyard in Soho by Christopher Nevinson and Mark Gertler. Artistic associations were also visible at the more up-market Pagani's, where the Artists' Room was lined with panels signed by painters, writers and musicians; at the Café Royal; and at Romano's in the Strand, which advertised itself as 'The Home of Bohemia' and was particularly associated with the theatre world.

The often rhapsodic descriptions of the Soho restaurant scene before World War One vividly convey a sense of its thrilling exoticism. Inevitably the atmosphere altered: 'The war ... gave Soho a boom period, and ... it lost its own personal note and became anybody's place. The suburbs and the provinces invaded it'.[11] What was regretted by the cognoscenti was welcomed by the restaurateurs, and the 1920s and 1930s saw Soho grow from strength to strength, trading on exactly the same factors that had appealed to the bohemians in the first place. By the 1930s a five-course *table d'hôte* meal was still modestly priced, and 'couples who couldn't afford a trip to Paris got "atmosphere", Continental food and charmingly broken English for a few shillings'.[12] Famous Soho restaurants founded between the wars included La Isola Bella (1923), Au Jardin des Gourmets (1931), and the Hungaria opened in 1928.

If fashion was one explanation of the irresistible advance of the restaurant, another was the arrival of a new breed of large restaurants, operated by caterers rather than by individual cooks. The prototype was the mammoth Criterion, which opened in 1874 offering a complex of eating rooms. It was joined in 1896 by the Trocadero, the flagship restaurant of the newly incorporated Jo Lyons & Co. Ltd, and in 1899 by the Brasserie de l'Europe, with its German Lager Hall, French Café and Italian Restaurant. These monster restaurant complexes were designed with a luxurious rather than a bohemian feel and they provided luxury on an unintimidating scale; thus extending the appeal of 'the restaurant dinner' to middle-class Londoners who might not have felt comfortable hiring a private room at either the Hotel Cecil or La Tour Eiffel. Further down the social ladder, Lyons Corner Houses, the first of which opened in Coventry Street in 1909, followed by branches in the Strand in 1915 and Oxford Street in 1928, supplied gilt and marble halls on a more modest scale.

Increased popularity for all types of restaurants was deeply bound up with the greater visibility of women eating in public. One development that depended absolutely on the presence of women was the addition of dancing to dining. Before World War I a few West End bars and luxury hotels had employed orchestras, but generally 'dancing at dinner in the better restaurants was an insanity not then thought of'.[13] The real craze for dancing burst on London after the war, with the sensational arrival of jazz in 1919 and the frantic hedonism of the bright young things. By the end of the 1920s most luxury restaurants and hotels had added dance floors and employed jazz bands, to compete with the new large 'dance restaurants' such as the Kit-Cat, which opened in 1927 in the Haymarket.

Dancing was not the only form of restaurant entertainment. The Kit-Cat offered cinema between courses. Many of the suburban road houses that sprung up in the 1920s to service the bright young things in motor cars offered all-night swimming pools. Cabaret appeared, as did night-clubs, most famously the Cave of the Golden Calf opened by Madame Strindberg in 1912. Many lamented this dilution of dining: 'Cabaret … is more important than cuisine, and the gourmet is a disappearing type.… Dining must be worked in with other things – with dancing and a show; and sitting over the port when you might be dancing is regarded as a waste of that time which nobody seems to have'.[14] The replacement of 'the restaurant dinner' by 'the evening out' fixed eating and food firmly in the sphere of pleasurable entertainment rather than functional necessity, a position well suited to the social and cultural changes that came later in the century.

By the 1930s, gastronomic expertise had reasserted itself. Marcel Boulestin's Restaurant Français opened in Leicester Square in 1925 and removed to Covent Garden in 1927 where it became the Restaurant Boulestin.[15] Boulestin can justifiably be called the first modern celebrity chef. Besides offering diners authentic French *haute cuisine*, as opposed to the bourgeois and often Italianate version found in Soho, Boulestin wrote a cookery column in *Vogue*, ran a cookery school at Fortnum & Masons and in 1937 became the nation's first television chef when he recorded the

67. 'Thè au Lyons' by Charles Laborde (1880–1941), one of the charming illustrations for *Rues et Visages de Londres*, a folio of hand-coloured etchings with text by Pierre MacOrlan, Paris (1928).

BBC's first cookery programme. It is thanks to Boulestin that a generation of English men and women were brought up to believe that the test of a good restaurant is the quality of its omelettes.

Boulestin's restaurant was also celebrated for its 'modern Parisian' interior design, with panels painted by Jean Laboureur and Marie Laurencin, and fabric designed by Raoul Dufy. Boulestin's set a tone of light modern chic that others were to follow in preference to the heavy and rich Belle Epoque styles that characterised the older luxury restaurants. Restaurants in the Boulestin mode of fine cuisine and smart design included Quaglinos, opened in 1929, Prunier's, opened in 1934 as a branch of the famous Paris restaurant, and Fischer's restaurant in Bond Street, opened in 1932 with interiors designed by Raymond McGrath.

THE TEA-SHOP AND DAYTIME EATING

If the restaurant came to dominate evening eating, so the tea-shop came to dominate the daytime, and like the restaurant everyone agreed that the spread of these new institutions was remarkable: 'it actually did, as many innovations falsely claim to do, fill a want which had been felt not only by women but by numbers of men of the City-office class, who were tired of the eating house and the public house.'[16]

The tea-shop trade was dominated by two large firms, the Aerated Bread Co., and Jo Lyons & Co., which opened its first tea-shop in Piccadilly in 1894. A host of smaller caterers, such as Appendrodt, Pearce and Plenty, Slaters and the Express Dairy Company, all served similar light lunch and teatime refreshments. Lyons tea-shops, like their Corner House restaurants, provided gilt and marble surroundings for all. They were enjoyed for their simplicity – no tipping; their female waitresses – the famous 'Nippies'; and their democratic classlessness.

The sandwich emerged as a lunchtime staple. Sweeting's, the old City fish restaurant, had installed a self-service sandwich counter by 1918. By the 1920s the first sandwich chain had appeared with Sandy's All British Sandwich Bars offering 60 varieties at 4d to 6d: 'no shellfish, no tinned food, no foreign produce, no tips, no waiting'.[17] By the 1930s lunch could also be soup, thanks to the Black and White Milk Bars, a stylish chain serving milk drinks and twenty-five varieties of soup, 'rich and pure in every way – 4d for a large bowl with oyster crackers'.[18] Light midday meals were also provided by vegetarian and 'food reform' restaurants, with at least five in

operation by 1918. The restaurant critic Newnham-Davis visited the Eustace Mills Restaurant in Chandos Street and reported that his fellow diners were 'ladies who might be stenographers or country cousins up for a day's shopping, young men who, I dare say, are bank clerks'.[19] On an earlier visit to a vegetarian café in St Martin's Lane he had had the *table d'hôte* of soup, flageolets, duck's eggs, salad, cheese and fruit for 1s 10d and 'went forth feeling rather empty'.[20]

Daytime eating establishments also included the department store restaurant and the East End café. The former was a 19th-century innovation, which grew in importance with the growing passion for shopping. By the 1920s all the central London stores were fully equipped with grill rooms and restaurants, providing snacks or meals at all hours in an ambience that flattered the shopper. By contrast, the ambience in the traditional East End eating-house remained firmly orientated to the working man, as did the food: 'Jumbo's joints are good, and so are his steak-toad, sprouts and baked, but his steak and kidney puddings at four pence are better. I had one of these with "boiled and tops". George had "leg, well done, chips and batter".'[21]

In the East End, as with the West End, change was driven by the Italians; in the 1920s and 1930s a new type of café, combining eating-house, milk bar and tea room

68. A 1930s photograph of the Black and White Milk Bar in Fleet Street. All branches of this distinctively styled chain had twenty-four hour opening, ideally suited to the newspaper industry, then concentrated in Fleet Street.

69. The interior of a Lyons Tea-shop in Leadenhall Street in the 1950s. The style of the interior is modern, clean and respectable.

70. The interior of a Wimpy Bar in South Kensington in 1968, a photograph by Henry Grant (b.1907). The brick walls and modern art marked a step forward in design from the American diner look of the original 1950s Wimpy Houses.

all in one, began to appear in the better class East End neighbourhoods. One celebrated example is Pellici's in Bethnal Green Road, opened in 1926 as an ice-cream parlour and furnished in the 1940s with inlaid wood panelling, still there today.

What of those to whom even a bun in a tea-shop was a luxury? Predictably, eating out is absent in the working-class Lambeth families described by Maud Pember Reeves in her classic study of 1913.[22] The families she looked at were not the poorest, in that the men were wage earners, yet eating out was unfamiliar, apart from the man's midday meal near his place of work. The same picture emerges from an equivalent study in 1939, which recognised in addition the 'social starvation' that afflicted women whose lives were bound up with the struggle to feed their families: 'they need to meet their fellows, to form social ties, to talk and laugh, and to eat food that they have not cooked themselves'.[23] It was to combat social starvation as much as malnutrition that the pioneering Peckham Health Centre of 1935 designed a self-service cafeteria into its facilities. The salads and sandwiches supplied there, and at equivalent social clubs and settlements, will have provided the only experience of eating out for many Londoners before World War II.

POST-WAR EATING: AMUSING FOOD

In the second half of the century, Londoners continued to eat out according to the patterns and trends set in the first. Luxury restaurants and hotels catered for the very rich; Soho provided continental food and ambience for all comers; the Boulestin tradition of serious *haute cuisine* in small restaurants was kept alive by Le Caprice, taken over by Mario Gallati in 1947, by Egon Ronay's Marquee in 1952, and by Le Gavroche, opened by the Roux Brothers in 1967. Light refreshments continued to flourish, albeit with changes of style, as the Black and White milk bars gave way to Charles Forté's red and white stripes: grill rooms became steak houses, and Corner Houses replaced their gilt and marble interiors with Formica and pine panelling. And as new target audiences were identified by the restaurant industry, which now started to turn its attention to children, having met the needs of women, so the eating-out habit continued to spread into hitherto untouched sectors of London's population.

Change, if not fundamental, was nevertheless noticeable, and post-war change will be looked at here in two broad ways. First, the growing importance of novelty and fun as ingredients in eating out, a trend that was particularly strong in the 1960s and which affected many types of restaurant from fast-food franchises to bistros in Chelsea catering for the in-crowd. The second broad change was the arrival of a genuine multi-cultural cuisine, the true foundation of London's current claim to be the restaurant capital of the world.

Underpinning both is a subtle cultural shift which affected almost every aspect of eating out over this period; the acceptance of informality as an appropriate mode of public behaviour. This found expression in the rise of the bistro, or the trattoria, both signifying something less formal than a restaurant; in the enthusiasm for what had once been street or snack food – such as pizza or Bhel Poori dishes; and in the fashion for eating outside on the pavement, as introduced to London by the Venus Kebab House in Charlotte Street in 1969. All combined to make eating out part of everyday life, rather than an extraordinary treat for which formal dress and behaviour were necessary.

The term 'amusing food' was coined by the writer Gregory Houston Bowden to describe the food created by a new breed of 1950s restaurants, located mainly in Belgravia and Chelsea and catering for a generation seeking modern novelty. The food in these new, trendy restaurants 'bent all the accepted rules and gave scope to the chef's imaginative talents',[24] with eccentrically British flair. The restaurants included The Ox on the Roof, opened in 1950, where diners were handed a table-sized menu and whose speciality, 'Millionaires Salad', combined Brazilian palm-tree hearts with shrimps; Le Matelot, whose interior was decorated with fish nets studied with fairy lights: La Bicyclette, where the speciality was chicken in a basket; La Popote, where Bill Stoughton created 'Scampi Bill'; and Parkes Restaurant, birthplace of garlic bread and the idea of describing dishes by amusing names such as 'Utter Bliss' or 'Ugly Ugly Duckling'– a half duckling surrounded with peaches, chestnuts and apricots.

Novelty of a less eccentric kind was provided by a new generation of continental eating places: the 'King's Road Mediterranean' style of bistros and trattorias. London's first bistros appeared in the early 1950s.[25] The best-known trattoria was Terrazza in Soho, opened in 1959, whose amusing talking point was an indoor vine with plastic grapes. The 1960s trattorias were different from their Soho predecessors in that the food was more assertively Italian; they sometimes offered particular regional cuisines, sometimes 'peasant food'; but all provided a more 'authentic' Italian taste than the often 'anglofied' dishes served up before the war. In similar fashion, and partly encouraged by diners who had absorbed the Elizabeth David gospel of Mediterranean food, Spanish restaurants became more assertively Spanish and Greek restaurants more genuinely Greek.

Design was of course a powerful tool in turning restaurants into amusing, attractive places, and some of the most adventurous design work of the 1950s and 1960s was carried out by large catering companies in imitation of American restaurant chains. Jo Lyons brought the hamburger to Britain with its Wimpies, introduced in 1953, initially through grill corners in existing Corner Houses, but then through special Wimpy Houses, of which there were eight or nine in Oxford Street alone by 1969. The Wimpy spread through the then novel technique of franchising, to which design was of course critical. Lyons employed design firms to style its various speciality outlets, which by the mid-1960s included Bacon, Egg and Mini-Steak Houses, Grill and Cheese restaurants, London Steak Houses and Chips with Everything, aimed at the youth market, whose Chancery Lane branch had a groovy pop art façade designed by Michael Wolff of Main Wolff and Partners.

The Golden Egg chain was also conscious of design. Its early restaurants by David Brookbank mixed American brashness, such as egg-shaped menus, with elements of modernist good taste, such as ceramic door pulls by the potter William Newland.

71. Chips with Everything, the façade of a Lyons restaurant at 88 Chancery Lane, aimed at the young and designed by Michael Wolff: 'the décor was conceived, according to the designer, in terms of a "pin-table aesthetic" – so everything is neon-lit in combinations of egg yellow, ketchup red and electric blue, and deafening music is provided by a giant juke box' (*Len Deighton's London Dossier*, 1967).

Design magazine approved the trend if not the results: 'the point is that the values now going into the restaurant interiors are design values, however crudely expressed'.[26] Peter Boizet's Pizza Express restaurants, the first of which opened in Wardour Street in March 1965, used design to appeal to a more sophisticated taste, with Eduardo Paolozzi murals in an early Fulham Road branch, and, more influentially, a crisp and stylish, white-tiled look created by Enzo Apicella along the lines of his redesign of Terrazza, where by the late 1960s the mural of Vesuvius and the vine with plastic grapes had been replaced with something much smarter.

Design took on even greater prominence with the arrival of the American prototypes from which Wimpies and Golden Eggs had learnt their techniques. London's first Kentucky Fried Chicken opened in North Finchley in November 1968. In October 1974 the first British McDonald's opened in Woolwich, followed rapidly by branches in Holloway, Catford and Croydon. McDonald's success was built on a very clear vision of inclusiveness, a message underlined by low prices, the bright and happy corporate look, and the child-friendly, easy-to-clean interiors, designed to free British families from what market research had identified as extraordinary shame and embarrassment associated with eating out with children. Families were McDonald's principal market, and with Greater London's captive market of nearly twelve million people the company initially concentrated on the suburbs. By 1978 the number of restaurants in the London area had increased to twenty-five, but the company reckoned the area could take over 100. As a result, 'London looks like keeping them busy for the next few years and there are no immediate plans to go outside the area'.[27]

POST-WAR EATING: ETHNIC FOOD

The presence of ethnic food in London was nothing new. What did become new in post-war London was the sheer number of ethnic restaurants, and the diversity of choice within any one cuisine, offering everything from street food to *haute cuisine*. Numbers of ethnic restaurants increased steadily from the late 1940s, but the 1970s was the decade when ethnic restaurants could be said to have acquired critical mass, their new found importance marked in 1975 when the *Good Food Guide* recommended as 'Best Value in London' the tiny Diwana Bhel Poori in Drummond Street. The Bhel Poori summed up all that was irresistible about ethnic restaurants: they were inexpensive, they were exotic, and they offered genuinely new tastes and dishes – the Bhel Poori sold vegetarian Gujerati street food, including the then novelties of 'Thali' platters and the Indian ice cream 'kulfi'.

The post-war change in status of ethnic restaurants can be measured by the movement of restaurants to and from the West End. Chinese cuisine provides a model of movement 'up town'. Although the West End had a solitary Chinese café, The Cathay, from 1908, Chinese restaurants were confined to the East End, where a community had settled near Limehouse. To most Londoners these East End Chinese restaurants represented an unpalatable 'other'. Yet by the 1940s the food had become

popular, and enterprising Chinese chefs had bought cheap property in the West End. By 1947: 'all over Soho you will find Chinese restaurants, varying from chop-suey joints to enormous well-appointed eating parlours. There is nothing sinister about them; indeed the clientele is more Anglo Saxon or American than Chinese'.[28] The success of large restaurants such as Ley On in Wardour Street and The Hong Kong on Shaftesbury Avenue led to further growth and to the formal establishment of 'China Town' by Westminster City Council in 1984 in south Soho.

By contrast Soho's Jewish restaurants in the same period catered not for the English but for a clientele that remained 99 per cent Jewish.[29] Soho supported a large Jewish community in those days, and its restaurants included Goody's in Berwick Street, 'England's oldest kosher restaurant', and Folman's off Wardour Street, 'the largest Jewish restaurant in England'. Kosher Jewish food never broke into the wider market, as Chinese food had done, and with the dispersal of the Jewish community from Soho so the restaurants went with them, as did those in London's Jewish East End, where the last, the famous Bloom's on Whitechapel High Street, closed in 1994.

72. 'Where the Fare includes Fried Noodle, Sharks' Fins, Sea Slugs, and Savouries of Bamboo Shoots: A typical Eating House in the Chinese Quarter of the East End' by S. Begg for *The Illustrated London News*, 10 January 1920. Although emphasising the unfamiliarity of the food the article also notes that the restaurant is clean and that non-Chinese diners are made welcome.

Indian food, albeit in simplified form as 'the curry', had the advantage of a familiarity developed through trading and colonial links. Between the wars a few Indian restaurants appeared in the West End, notably Veeraswamy's, which opened in Regent Street in 1925 following the owner's success running the Indian café at the British Empire Exhibition at Wembley. Others arrived post-war – two examples are Jamshids from the 1950s and The Punjab Restaurant in Neal Street, which opened in 1968, both providing sophisticated Indian cuisine for the curry cognoscenti. But the real breakthrough came with the arrival in the 1970s of the Bangladeshi community, bringing entrepreneurship and a post-colonial adventurousness. Bengali-run curry houses began to proliferate on London's suburban streets, while Indian cuisine began to move in new directions with the restaurateur Amin Ali, who opened his pioneering 'Last Days of the Raj' in 1977 followed by Lal Qila in 1981 and the Red Fort in 1983. These restaurants represented a new generation of stylish and creative Indian restaurants, no longer aiming just to replicate 'authentic' food but moving the cuisine forward in a highly sophisticated way.

In the last twenty years of the century eating out in London has moved up a gear with a new and exuberant emphasis on both food and chef. London's chefs are now world class, acclaimed by the Michelin star standards of traditional *haute cuisine* and celebrated for their creativity. The capital has discovered a rich seam of genuinely food-orientated innovation, springing partly from *nouvelle cuisine*, which returned structure and composition to restaurant food after the shapeless Mediterranean stews of the 1960s, and partly by the new world of possibilities that ethnic cuisines brought with them. The last few years have also seen a new injection of entrepreneurial vigour, notably from Terence Conran, pioneer of London's stylish mega-restaurants with Quaglinos opened in 1993 and Mezzo in 1995.

The complexity of London's end-of-the-century restaurant scene is underlined by the lack of agreement over restaurant categories; what is 'New British' in one guide is 'Modern European' in another; The River Cafe is 'Evolved Italian'; Bam Bou, which occupies the historic Tour Eiffel site of 1 Percy Street, is Vietnamese but with a Parisian-trained chef who offers globally tinged Asian dishes and an international wine list. This site reflects many of the century's changes: beginning in 1908 as a French restaurant run by an Austrian chef, it then became London's leading Greek restaurant and now offers French-Vietnamese food using ingredients that were probably unfamiliar to Stulik himself let alone to his diners. No.1 Percy Street offers two broad conclusions about the last 100 years. First, change has been intimately bound up with immigrant talent; and secondly, change in eating out mirrors the unprecedented social, cultural and economic shifts that the century has seen.

73. Items from Pharmacy, opened in 1998 by a partnership which included the artist Damien Hirst, whose work set the tone of the restaurant's influential look and feel.

Left
74. Items from The Ivy. The menu cover is the work of Tom Phillips, one of many artists involved in the restaurant's refurbishment in 1990. Phillips also created a glass screen and wall of painted portraits in the interior.

Focus **Eating Out in Wartime** Cathy Ross

■

■

■

■

Eating out was as disrupted by war as any other aspect of daily life in London. In both world wars the broad effects were the same: private restaurants came under government regulations; food shortages curtailed the meals available; and the state entered the catering trade through National Kitchens in the World War One and the Londoners' Meal Service and British Restaurants in the Second.

Both wars bought mixed blessings to London's continental restaurants. They benefited from the influx of foreign nationals – refugees fleeing the conflict in

75. The 'Cost Price Restaurant' run by the East London Federation of Suffragettes at Old Ford, 1914. This suffragette initiative set up in August 1914 provided a two-course midday meal at 2d for adults and 1d for children. Soup was available between 7 and 8 pm at 1d a pint.

Europe, soldiers on 'relaxation and recreation' leave from the front or American and Canadian servicemen. Less happily, war also brought anti-foreign feeling. Schmidt's in Charlotte Street was one of several German restaurants forced to close at the outbreak of war in 1914 because of anti-German riots. During World War Two many of Soho's Italian waiters were interned, and some Italian restaurants diplomatically altered their allegiances to become French or Swiss.

Government intervention through rationing and controls also produced good and bad. Pricing controls on restaurant meals were introduced in 1942, largely through a

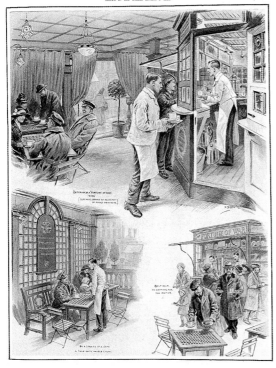

fear that the rich might buy their way out of rationing. No meal was to consist of more than three courses nor to cost more than five shillings, with exceptions for certain luxury restaurants. The five-shilling meal was said to 'hang like a sword of Damocles over every kitchen', according to Stanley Jackson in *An Indiscreet Guide to Soho*. But it had the effect for some diners of putting hitherto luxurious restaurants within their reach, as one

young Londoner discovered: 'I myself had always wanted to visit Prunier's legendary fish restaurant in St James's. I understood this to be a cut above our local fish and chip shop – and it was. My five shillings bought me a splendid dish of mussels. Madame Prunier came to my table to enquire whether it was satisfactory. And, as I left, I saw the Duke of Windsor sitting on a high stool at the bar'.[30] Surviving wartime menus from Prunier's show that the restaurant continued to provide its customers with luxurious dishes such as Lobster Thermidor. It also offered a take-away 'Black Out Dinner' costing twelve shillings and six pence.

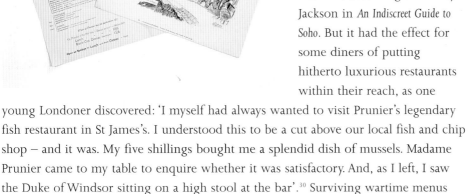

London Now

What are the secrets of London's restaurant success? New attitudes towards leisure, pleasure and status? The alliance between art, food and fashion? The skills of restaurant staff? Entrepreneurs and investors? These pictures record the complex excellence of London's restaurants today.

Far left
79. Quagino's, Bury Street SW1, 1999.

Above left
80. Phillip Makepeace, a Londoner eating out in Covent Garden, 1999.

Above right
81. Elena Salvoni is one of Soho's best-known restaurateurs. Born in London in 1920, she worked at Bianchi's and L'Escargot before opening Elena's Etoile in 1996.

Left
82. Kensington Place, Kensington Church Street W8, 1999

Equivalent contemporary values of the pound:
an historical series 1270 to 1999 compiled by the Bank of England

The figures are not seasonally adjusted								
£1	in	1270	=	£410.25	as	at	March	1999
£1	in	1320	=	£328.20	as	at	March	1999
£1	in	1370	=	£328.20	as	at	March	1999
£1	in	1420	=	£410.25	as	at	March	1999
£1	in	1470	=	£410.25	as	at	March	1999
£1	in	1520	=	£410.25	as	at	March	1999
£1	in	1570	=	£149.18	as	at	March	1999
£1	in	1620	=	£86.37	as	at	March	1999
£1	in	1670	=	£74.59	as	at	March	1999
£1	in	1720	=	£74.59	as	at	March	1999
£1	in	1770	=	£56.59	as	at	March	1999
£1	in	1820	=	£33.49	as	at	March	1999
£1	in	1870	=	£41.03	as	at	March	1999
£1	in	1920	=	£18.23	as	at	March	1999
£1	in	1970	=	£8.87	as	at	March	1999
£1	in	1975	=	£4.81	as	at	March	1999
£1	in	1980	=	£2.46	as	at	March	1999
£1	in	1985	=	£1.73	as	at	March	1999
£1	in	1990	=	£1.30	as	at	March	1999
£1	in	1995	=	£1.10	as	at	March	1999

This statistical series shows changes in the value of money over the past seven centuries and gives the amount of money required at March 1999 to purchase the goods bought by £1 at the dates shown on the table.

Thus, £74.59 would have been required in March 1999 in order to have the same purchasing power as £1 in 1670.

The figures are derived from the Retail Price Index, based at January 1987 = 100.

The RPI is based on the combined cost of a number of specific goods and does not take into account other factors relevant to a comparison of values: for example, the cost of real property or the level of wages. We know of no figures incorporating all possible factors.

Picture credits

Artothek Art Library: fig 8
Bridgeman Art Library: fig 10, fig 24, fig 44
British Architectural Library, RIBA, London: front cover, fig 66
British Museum: fig 28, fig 39, fig 49, Fig 62,© The British Museum
Courtauld Institute: fig 31© The Society of Dilletanti
Design Council Archive of the University of Brighton: fig 71, back cover
Fox Photos: fig 2, fig 68, fig 77
Frans Francken II: fig 3, German Bread Museum, Ulm
Guildhall Library: fig 5, fig 21, fig 25, fig 27, fig 40, fig 52, fig 55
Herzog Anton Ulrich Museum: fig 9
Maurithuis the Hague: fig 11, fig 26
Mercers' Company: fig 6, reproduced by courtesy of The Worshipful Company of Mercers'
Tate Gallery: fig 46, fig 65, reproduced by courtesy of the estate of John Roberts
Tower Hamlets Local History Library: fig 75
Wallraf Richartz Museum: fig 13

Footnotes

The 16th Century

1 Fisher, F.J., 1948, 'The Development of London as a Centre of Conspicuous Consumption in the Sixteenth and Seventeenth Centuries', *Transactions of the Royal Historical Society* (4th series), vol. 30, p. 37.

2 Stow, J., 1603 edn, *A Survey of London*, ed. C.L. Kingsford, 2 vols (Oxford), 1908, vol. ii 9 65; also 65, ii 35–9 and Harley Ms 544 fol. 98v; year given as 1521–22.

3 Rappaport, S., 1983, 'Social Structure in Sixteenth-Century London', part 1 (*London Journal*), vol. 9, no. 2, Winter, pp. 107–52.

4 Why is this? Archaeological excavations in London have produced abundant botanical and faunal evidence for the consumption of exotic, wild and domestic species but unfortunately none of the finds, usually recovered from cellars, wells and cesspits, can be directly attributed to eating-out establishments.

5 Stow, op. cit., vol. ii, p. 222.

6 Carlin, M., 1998, 'Fast Food and Urban Living Standards in Medieval England', p. 30, note 9, in Carlin, M., and Rosenthal, J.T., eds, *Food and Eating in Medieval Europe*, London.

7 Lydgate, J., mid-15th century, in 'London Lyckpeny'; cf. Harley Mss 367 and 542; also Stow, op. cit., 1598 edn.

8 Stow, op. cit., 1598, ii, pp. 222–3.

9 It is possible that the 'cookshop' is not a separate eating-out establishment but rather the kitchen of an inn or tavern.

10 Schofield, J., 1987 edn, 'The London Surveys of Ralph Treswell', London Topographical Society, publication no. 135, p. 20 and plate 7, from Christ's Hospital Evidence Book, 17, 1611.

11 Southwark, Lady Day Proc. G. Lib. Ms 6595 fol. 23, 1666.

12 Chaucer, G., 1386–9, *Canterbury Tales*, General Prologue, l 379–87, and Cook's Prologue, L 4344–51 in *Chaucer Complete Works*, Skeet, W.W., ed., Oxford, 1976, pp. 423–4 and 474.

13 Carlin, op. cit, chap. 3, pp. 27–51, in Carlin and Rosenthal, 1998, op. cit.

14 Shakespeare, W., *Henry V*, iii, 2. 81.

15 CLRO Com. Ser. Book 2, fol. 75B, Box 3, roll no. 406, William House, 29 May 1668; also Analytical Index to the series of records known as 'Rembrancia AD 1579–1664', London, 1878, iv, p. 544, roll no. 100, 10 February 1617 (Cook, Lythan Price purchased the lease of a house and shop in Southwark to set up a tippling house).

16 Borde, A.?, 1542, Regyment..., fol. G ii.

17 Dent, A., 1601, *The Plaine Mans Path-Way to Heaven*, p. 192, London; and 5 & 6 Edward VI, c.25 extended by 7 Edward VI, c.5; also *Short Title Catalogue of Books 1475–1640*, ed. Pollard, A.W., et al., 1926; various proclamations, nos 180, 19 January 1619.

18 'Rembrancia', op. cit., 111.126, 20 January 1613.

19 Zetzner, J.-E., 1700, *Londres et l'angleterre en 1700*, Strasbourg, 1905, p. 14; *The Diary of Samuel Pepys*; eds Latham, R. and Matthews, W., 10 vols, London, 1983; 17 January 1663.

20 Ward, E., 1698, *The London Spy* in Hayward, A.L., ed. London 1927, p. 25; and Harrison, W.,

1577, Description of England, Bk. ii, chap. vi, p. 161. ed. Funivall, F.J. Early English Text Society (EETS) 1878.

21 Pepys' *Diary*, op. cit., 22 June 1663.

22 CLRO, Alchin Papers, Box H/103/10, 1673, Victuallers Recognizance 14.

23 Pepys' *Diary*, op. cit., 24 May 1663.

24 Harrison, W., op. cit., 1576, chap. xv, p. 145. The wives of Liverymen were obliged to attend the feasts because they had good cause not to do so.

25 The Worshipful Company of Drapers' Wardens Accounts, 1566, 1569 and 1571.

26 Drapers' Company, ibid., Rep.7, p. 214; also Privy Council, 1522, 1593 and Rep. 7, p. 214.

27 The average labourer's wage in this period was about 6d.

28 Rappaport, op. cit., 1983, p. 124.

29 Drapers' Company, 1564 to 1602; £41 10s 3d to as much as £112 12s 6d (when the Master was Lord Mayor). Worshipful Company of Grocers' feasts were very modest in comparison, averaging £20.

30 Drapers' Company, Ms D.B. 1 (1564–1602).

31 It is equally possible that the smallest pike were reserved for the top tables because they may have had a better texture and flavour.

32 In 1516, the Drapers' had 78 guests; 30 members at the principal table, 100 at two side tables, 40 ladies at two tables in the ladies' chamber and 20 maidens in the Chequer Chamber; and in 1554, 89 guests were invited to the feast; 25 for the high table, including wives, and 32 each for the second and third tables. The Grocers' consumed 214 quail in 1511/12, so if those attending had one quail each, there were perhaps 214 altogether (pers. com. P. Siddell, Archivist of the Grocers' Company).

33 Comfits contained spices and whole seeds such as fennel, coriander and caraway.

34 Yellow and red from turnesole; yellow from sanders and gold leaf. Wafers were supplied by a couple of the officers' wives, and they were paid 2s a box (Drapers' Company Wardens' Accounts, 1576).

35 c.1520s from North America, in Stowe's Annals, Howes, E., ed., London, 1615, vol. 1, p. 948.

36 1607.

37 Magno, A., 1562. *The London Journal of Alessandro Magno*, 1562, eds Barron, C., et al, in *The London Journal*, vol. 9, no. 2, Winter 1983, pp. 141–52; also, Sorbiere, S., 1698, *A Journey to London in the Year 1698*, London, p. 29.

38 Harrison, op. cit., Book ii, p. 148.

39 Drapers' Company Accounts, 1564 and 1565.

40 Procs. 1563 and 1596, Cogan, T., 1596, *Haven of Health*, p. 39, note 1, in Furnivall, F.J., ed., 1908, EETS, ref. to Fish Days on Wednesday, Fridays and Saturdays; Drapers' Company Quarter Day Supper, 1570.

41 Eels were particularly popular, and various types are mentioned: Conger, Sand, Pimper and Stub.

42 Harrison, op. cit., 1576, 46 i. 52; also Stow, op. cit., 1598, vol I, p. 20 ref. to the 'great store of verie good fish' in the City Ditch during the early 16th century.

43 Andrewes, L., undated, in 'The Noble Lyfe &

Natures of man, Of bestes/Serpentys/flowles & fisshes yt be moste knowen', in Furnivall, op. cit., EETS, pp. 113–23.

44 Drapers' Company Wardens' Accounts; a Lenten Quarter Day Supper in 1570 included '4 olde linge and 4 green fyshes'; the preserved fish was more expensive at 3s each, compared with the fresh at 20d each.

45 Harrison, 1576, op. cit., 46. i. 52, p. 157; Grocers' Company Ms 11, 571/3; and this scarcity is reflected in the Drapers' accounts when carp was eaten three times between 1567 and 1570; cf. also Mascall, L., 1590, 'A Booke of Fishing with Hooke & Line' in Lever, C., 1977, *The Naturalized Animals of the British Isles*, London, p. 443.

46 Grocers' Company, Ms 11, 571/3, 1511–21. (I am very grateful to Mrs Pauline Siddell of the Grocers' for information on dining in the company archives; personal communication).

47 Personal communication, Alan Pipe (archaeozoologist, Museum of London), April 1999 and Richard Sabin (zoologist, B.M. Nat. Hist.).

48 Roxburghe Ballads, British Museum, printed 1560 and 1700; also Sorbiere, S., 1666, *Relation d'un voyage en Angleterre*, Cologne, pp. 149, 150; also PRO, SP 12/8, no. 31, 1559, and British Library Lansdowne Ms 8/17, 1564–5.

49 Harrison, op. cit., 1576, Book iii, chap. xv, p. 324.

50 Borde, A?, 1542, *A Compendyous Regyment or a Dyetary of Helth*, Furnivall, F.J., ed. EETS, E. S. 10, London, 1870 fol. H ii.

51 Russell, J., c.1430–70, *Boke of Nurture*, p. 72;.also Records of the Carpenters' Company Wardens' Accounts for the period 1438–1516.

52 Personal communication, Giorgi, J. (archeobotanist, Museum of London); barberry seeds have been recovered from a 16th-century dump at Finsbury Island Pavement. Plum stones are frequently found in archaeological contexts, the varying sizes suggesting the great number of varieties consumed in the period (cf. Parkinson, J., 1629, *Paridisi in sole Paradisus Terrestris*, listing 61 different types). There is only one possible find of quince from a mid- to 17th-century deposit at 4-12 Norton Folgate. Grape seeds are commonly found in London, but most of these were probably from imported dried fruit. Fig seeds are extremely common, and again many of these probably came from imported dried fruit.

53 Frans Franken II (1581–1642), oil on panel, 75 x 105 cm (30 x 42 in), German Bread Museum, Ulm.

54 Records of the Carpenters' Company Wardens' Accounts, vol. iv, 1570, p. 237 (p. 406), 'Paied for grapes ijd'.

55 Russell, op. cit., c.1430–70, p. 716; and Borde, A., Regyment, N.i.6, Of Prunes and Damysens.

56 Busino, O., 1618, 'Angliopotrida, as Englisht by Mr Rawdon Brown', in Harrison, part I, Furnivall, F.J., ed., op. cit. (on London Noises and Water, 1617–8), and Hentzner, P., 1698, *A journey into England in the year 1598*, trans. Bentley, R., Horace Walpole, ed., London, 1765.

57 Strawberries: Drapers' Company, 1570; Cherries: Drapers' Company, 1573/74 and

Grocers' Ms 11, 571/3, 1573–4.

58 Lydgate, mid-15th century, op. cit., *Roxburghe Ballads*, 9 vols, London, 1871–97, and Turner, W., in *A Dish of Stuff; or a Gallymonfery*, c.1600–20?

59 Busino, O., 1618, p. 61, in Harrison, part I, op. cit.

60 Occasional references: e.g. Records of the Carpenters' Company, vol. ii, 1514, fol. 175a.

61 da Confienza, P., 1477, *Summa Lacticimiorum (Trattato die Latticini)*, Turin, translation from Latin into Italian, Milan, 1990, chap. 12; the author would like to thank Gillian Rilley for this information.

62 In 1559, £2,482 13s 4d of Dutch cheese was imported into London, cf. PRO. SP/12/8, no. 31, 1559.

63 Brown and rye bread were consumed by the poorer classes, cf. Harrison, op. cit. Book ii, chap. vi, pp. 154–5.

64 Russell, op. cit., c.1430–70, Harley Ms, 4011, fol. 171.

65 Drapers' Company, Jan. 1564/5, 6d for 2 days' work.

66 Pl. 6, Clothworkers' Company Plan Book, 10-11, 1612, in Schofield, J., op. cit. 1987.

67 *Pepys' Diary*, op. cit., 29 October 1663.

68 A great deal of City plate was melted down during the Civil War for bullion.

69 Johnson, A. H., *The History of the Worshipful Company of the Drapers of London*, vols 1–5, Oxford, 1914.

70 1567 Lottery, Cook's Motto, Loseley Mss, 1567, p. 50, in Phillips, F.T., *Worshipful Company of Cooks of London*, London, 1966.

71 Drapers' Company Wardens' Accounts 1569, 1570 &c. 6 June, 1570, 7 August, 1570; 1580; also 'Court of Husting', London G Lib Mss, roll 247–129, 23 March 1554, pp. 656–7.

72 Cogan, T., 1596, 'Haven of Health', in Furnivall, op. cit., 1868, p. 38; and Russell, op. cit., c.1430–70, 79/1182.

73 Russell, op. cit., c.1430–70, 33/505–508.

74 White, T., 1577, *On West of Charity*, 3 November, p. 65, a sermon preached at 'Paules Cross', Furnivall, ed., op cit., part ix, supplement.

75 1568. *Institucion of a Gentleman*, Whittingham, C., ed.,1839; cf. Heal, F., *Hospitality in Early Modern England*, Oxford, 1990, p. 116.

76 Harrison, op. cit., Book iii, chap. vi, p.144.

77 'Court of Husting', G Lib. Ms. roll 247 (129, 23 March, 1554)

Focus

78 Greene, R, 1588, *Perimedes the blacke-smith: a golden methode...* London; Addison, J., *The Spectator*, No. 251, Tues, 18th December; Gay, J., 1716, *Trivia*; Ward, E., op. cit., p. 100; *Roxburghe Ballads*, 8 vols.

79 Gorson, S., 1580, *Playes Confuted and School of Abuse*; Hetzner, P., 1598, in Horace Walpole's *Englishing*, 1757, p. 41–3

80 Howard, J., 1674, *The English Mounsieur: A comedy...*; Ward, E., 1699, *Walk to London* fol. ii, 63, ff.ed. 1709, *Islington Wells, or the Threepenny Academy*, 1691; Wither, G., 1628, *Brittain's Remembrancer*.

81 Ward, E., op.cit., p. 100; and Dunn, J., 1601, *Entertainment, a Comedy*.

82 GL Ms 20, 821.

83 Worshipful Company of Grocers', 1 October 1617, pageant expenses £5 7s 8d.

84 1710, Ashton, p. 219, Notes & Querries, 12th ser. 10, 1922, 331; von Uffenbach, Z.C., 1710, London, in 1710 from *The Travels of Zacharias Conrad van Uffenbach*, trans. and ed. W.H. Quarrell and M. Mare, London, p. 4.

85 van Etten, H. 1633, *Mathematical Recreations*, LXXIIII, London, pp. 128–9.

86 Ashton, J., 1883, p. 219, *Social Life of Queen Anne*, London; Daily Courant, 14 August 1703.

The 17th Century

1 James I complained that the gentry, in pursuit of urban pleasures, were neglecting their country estates and thereby, the rural economy.

2 Gay, J., 1716, *Trivia: or, the art of walking the streets of London*; also 'The English Lady's Catechism', 1703, pamphlet, J. A., 'I hate everything that Old England bringe forth. I love the French Bread, French wines, French sauces and a French Cook'.

3 Misson, H., 1698, *Memoirs and Observations in his Travels over England*, trans. Ozell, 1719, p. 313.

4 *The Basset Table*; and Rees, R.N., and Fenby, C., 1931, 'Meals and Mealtimes', in Reginald Lennard, ed., *Englishmen at Rest and Play*, Oxford.

5 Misson, op. cit., 1698, p. 314.

6 G Lib., Anon, Pam. 1920; 1675, *The Character of a Tavern with a brief draught of a Drawer*, London.

7 Harrison, op. cit., 1576, clxvi, p. 109; Magno, op. cit., 1562, p. 141: the Ball Inn (possibly on the north side of Lombard Street, p. 150 note 4) was run by an Italian proprietor.

8 Ward, E., 1698, op. cit., p. 71; the Rose Tavern sold fine claret.

9 CLRO, Com. Ser. roll 17, 30 September 1661, sign and post valued at £16. Several tavern signs were destroyed by Whig youths on 6 November 1682, including the Cardinal's Head sign in Cheapside. CLRO Sessions File, December 1682.

10 Zetzner, J.-E., 1700, *Londres et L'angleterre en 1700*, Strasbourg, 1905, p. 14.

11 Larkin, J.F., and Hughes, P.L., eds, *Stuart Royal Proclamations*, vol. i, Oxford, 1973; 1 Jac.I.c.9 [1603–4]; Presentment 1599–1600.

12 Taylor, J., 1637, G Lib. Pam. 2458, 'The Carriers Cosmographie or A Briefe Relation of the Innes, Ordinaries, Hosteries and other lodgings in, and neere London, where the Carriers, Waggons, Foote-posts and Higglers, doe usually come, from any parts'.

13 Keene, D., 1985, *Cheapside before the Great Fire*, London, 1985; *Pepys' Diary*, op. cit., 8 June 1661.

14 CLRO, Com. Ser. Box 52, roll 17, 30 September 1661; innkeeper William Longe of Marylebone had 17 sheep, 15 ducks and 24 pigeons as well as a bowling green, garden and arbours; the Fox Tavern in King Street, Westminster, had 4 hearths with a garden.

15 *Pepys' Diary*, op. cit., 11 December 1661.

16 CLRO, Com. Ser. Book 5, box 32, fol. 19B, 2256, John Carter, Vintner, 20 April 1697; Com. Ser. Book 5, Box 31, fol. 11, 2234, Simon Smith, Vintner, 8 November 1695; Com. Ser. Book 4, box 27, fol. 229B, 2202, George Mason, 7 July 1685.

17 CLRO MIS 1C/151/3; The Crown was also regularly used by the parish of St Christopher-le-Stocks for audit day and accession day dinners.

18 Pearl, V., 1979, Cornhill, p. 160 (wards are administrative divisions within the City of London).

19 Zetzner, op. cit.; and *Pepys' Diary*, op. cit.,1 October 1660, at the Miter; and 19 March 1660.

20 *Pepys' Diary*, op. cit., 17 October 1660 – The Feathers in Fish Street.

21 *Pepys' Diary*, op. cit., 15 March 1661.

22 *Pepys' Diary*, op. cit., 3 July 1662.

23 Zetzner, op. cit., p. 15.

24 CLRO City Cash Accounts, 1/1, 32–5.

25 G Lib Broadside, 24.67, no. 61, 1641, 'An Exact Legendary compendiously containing the whole life of Alderman Abel'.

26 Misson, 1698, op. cit., p. 69.

27 Stow, op cit., 1598, I, p. 83.

28 1,587 licensed; 7 Edward VI, c.5 [1553]; CLRO Letter Book R, fol. 268v; and CLRO ref. Cust. 14, fols 242v and 243r; 'Rembrancia', op. cit.; V27, 25 September 1618; ref. 10 July 1612; III, 54; Alexander, J.M.B., 1989, unpulished PhD thesis, LSE, 4 vols, *Economic and Social Structure of the City of London*, c.1700, p. 136.

29 CLRO P.D.10.112, 8 May 1695; and similar Orders on 13 May 1698, P.D.10.113; and 10 January, 1700/1.P.D.10.114.

30 CLRO 'Rembrancia', op. cit., 10 July 1612, III.54, and 8 October 1633, VII 94.

31 Burnaby, A., 1690, *An Essay upon the Exercising of Malt*, p. 76, London.

32 *Pepys' Diary*, op. cit., 1 August 1660.

33 *Pepys' Diary*, op. cit., 1 September 1660 and 18 May 1668.

34 Ward, op. cit., 1698, p. 4.

35 *Pepys' Diary*, op. cit., 10 December 1662.

36 *Pepys' Diary*, op. cit., 9 November 1660.

37 G Lib. Broadside 24.61, 1641, no. 61: Fridays observed as Fish Days.

38 CLRO MISC/86/8, 29 October 1673.

39 CLRO MISC/86/8.

40 Taylor, J., op. cit., 1618,. Aldersgate Street, Cripplegate and New Fish Street.

41 Ward, op. cit, 1698, p. 158, *Vanburgh's Relapse*.

42 *Pepys' Diary*, op. cit., 16 February 1660.

43 *Pepys' Diary*, op. cit., 2 March 1660; 2 October 1660.

44 Dekker, T., 1609, *Gull's Horn-Book*, chap. v, London.

45 *Pepys' Diary*, op. cit., 12 May 1667.

46 Stuart Royal Proclamations, vol. I, 6 February 1619, p. 424, etc.; Powell, T., 1631, *Tom All Trades*, p. 141; also Garrard to Lord Strafford (Strafford Papers, vol. I, p. 21) 3 June 1634; and Cartwright, W., 1651, *A Comedy*, 1651, London.

47 *Pepys' Diary*, op. cit., 24 June 1661.

48 *Pepys' Diary*, op. cit., 10 May 1663; Very Rev. R. Davies's Journal; Knowles, W., 'The Earl of Strafforde's Letter and Dispatches' in Garrard, 1739. In a letter to Wentworth, 1634, concerning the high price of the Ordinary in Spring Gardens, Strafforde suggests that some form of pricing regulation had been introduced for Ordinaries, the standard being 2s. The present author has not found any extant legislation to support this.

49 *Pepys' Diary*, op. cit., 4 July 1663.

50 *Pepys' Diary*, op. cit., 7 May 1661.

51 *Pepys' Diary*, op. cit., 22 October 1660 and 19 May 1661.

52 G. Lib. Ms 6595, fol. 19.

53 Alexander, 1989, op. cit., vol. 4, map 6.28, showing the distribution of Cooks throughout the city, p. 304.

54 Carlin, op. cit., pp. 25–5.

55 Ward, op. cit., 1698, pp. 86–7.

56 Ward, op. cit., 1698, p. 184.

57 Ward, op. cit., 1698, pp. 93–4.

58 Misson, op. cit., 1698, pp. 145–6.

59 Zetzner, op. cit., p. 16; Misson, op. cit., 1698, pp. 313–4.

60 OED reference 1690. B.E. Dict. Cant. Crew, Chop-houses, 'where both boyld and roast mutton (in chopps) are alwayes ready'.

61 Zetzner suggests as many spits as 15–20, p. 16.

62 CLRO Com. Ser. Book 2, fol. 356, 1005, 22 October 1674; Book 5, fol. 20.2258, 2 rolls, 25 March 1690; Book 2, 453, fol. 96B, 3 February 1660; Com. Ser. Book 2, fol. 75B, 406, 29 May 1668.

63 Zetzner, op. cit., 1700, p. 16.

64 Pepys' Diary, op. cit., 2 October 1661; 17 October 1661; 23 May 1661 and 12 January 1663.

65 Smollett, T., 1748, Roderick Random, pp. 102–3.

66 Magno, op. cit., 1562, p. 143.

67 Stow, op. cit., 1598, vol. I, pp. 301 and 165; Museum of London Copperplate Map c.1559.

68 Brown, T., 1700, Amusements Serious and Comical, part ii, 'The Thames'.

69 Garrard to Lord Strafford, 3 June 1634, in Strafford Papers, op. cit., vol. i, p. 262.

70 Strafford Papers, ibid., 24 June 1635, and Augmentation Records, no. 73, 1650, 'A Survey of Certain Lanes and Tenements, scituate and being at Pickadilley, the Blue Muse and others thereunto adioyninge'.

71 Misson, op. cit., 1698, p. 39.

72 CLRO Journal 48, fol. 189, Order of Common Council, December 1675; Ward, op. cit., 1698, p. 218; 'The Grand Concern of England Explained', 23 December 1675; Proclamation, Charles II, 8 January 1676, and Lillywhite, B., London Coffee Houses, London, 1963, no. 556.

73 British Museum, undated, c.1655.

74 cf. The Intelligencer, 19–26 May 1657; Bartholomew Lane Coffee-House.

75 House of Commons, Order of Council 1660.

76 CLRO Alchin Papers, Box H/103/12.

77 CLRO Com. Ser. Book 2. fol. 78. 414, 11 April 1668; G Lib. Ms 1903, June 1695 and 20 September 1690; Nandoes Coffee house, 15 Fleet Street, 21 December 1657; Wardmote Inquest, Lillywhite, op. cit., 1043 – Rainbow, Fleet Street. Coffee-houses established before 1700 for which evidence survives number 251 (by the author's calculation).

78 All Coffee-houses were required to be licensed from 1663 for a fee of 12d.

79 CLRO Misc. Mss 95.10; Morat's Coffee-House in Exchange Alley. Lillywhite, op. cit., 838 established in 1662 and 1157, ref. to Sam's Coffee House in Ave Maria Lane (Hampstead wells water); Mercurius Publicus. 12–19 March 1662.

80 CLRO P.D. 10,112; 133 and 114; Alexander, op. cit., 1989, Poll Tax Assessments 1692.

81 Don Saltero's Chelsea, cf. Lillywhite, op. cit., 352, 169; and 465; The Intelligencer, 21 December 1663; The Commonwealth Mercury, 2 September 1658.

82 The Character of a Coffee-House, by an Eye and Ear Witness, 1665, London.

83 Lillywhite, op. cit., 1963, no. 1548, Will's Coffee-House, Covent Garden; London Gazette, 1693, no. 2957.

84 Ward, op. cit., 1698, p. 10.

85 The Coffee Club, New Palace Yard, Westminster - cf. Aubrey's ref. to a purposely made 'large

oval table, with a passage in the middle, for Miles to deliver his Coffee'. cf. Lillywhite, op. cit., no. 263, 1659–60.

86 CLRO Box 50, Book 6. fol. 134B, 3315.

87 G Lib. Mss Add. 1063–70, 7 August 1700; CLRO Com. Ser. Book G, fol. 317, 2211, 11 November, 1691.

88 The Spectator, no. 49; Ward, op. cit., 1698, Nadoes'(Coffee House, p. 218; CLRO Sessions Report.

89 Pepys' Diary, op. cit., 30 March 1668; also curious ref. to 'spent at ye coffee-house on ye children – Lillywhite, op. cit., no. 1011 – from Parish Account books ref. 1683 - Barge Yard; St Stephen's Walbrook Vestry Minutes, 29 April 1680.

90 The Poll Tax Assessments for 1692 show that 32 out of 137 coffee-houses in London were run by women – Alexander, op. cit., 1989, and Lillywhite, op. cit., no. 1167; Sarah's Coffee house, Cheapside, 1699, Court Book of the East India Company, vol. xxxvii, Ap. 167. Brown, op. cit., 1700, refers to Coffee-house/brothels where a 'Charming Phillis or two…invite you by their amorous glances into their smoaky Territories', p. 130.

91 The author has not found any contemporary evidence to support this contention and the earliest reference in the OED is for 1755. cf. Ukers, W.H., 1922 and 1935, All about Coffee, chap. ix, p. 69, and Twining, S.H., 1956, The House of Twining 1706–1956, London, p. 6.

92 April 27/30, 1706.

93 Zetzner, op. cit., 1700, p. 17; Pepys' Diary, 26 April 1661.

Focus

94 Boswell, J., 1791, The Life of Johnson, reprint, ed. Christopher Hibbert, Harmondsworth, 1979, p. 212.

95 Tonson Mss, National Portrait Gallery, cited in Douglas Stewart, J., 1971, Sir Godfrey Kneller, London, p. iii.

96 Percy, S., 1821, Annals of the Fine Arts, 'Obit.', p. 177, quoted in Pyke, E.J., 1973, A Biographical Dictionary of Wax Modellers, Oxford, p. 105.

The 18th Century

1 Anon., 1768, The Art of Living in London, a Poem, London, for W. Griffin, J. Kearsley and F. Newbury, canto I.

2 Strype, John, 1720, Survey of London, III, p. 207.

3 CLRO, Orphan's Inventory, roll 3073; Inventory of William Bricknell, Innholder, 1719, London.

4 Pearce, J. (forthcoming), A late 18th-century Inn Clearance from Uxbridge, Middlesex.

5 Maclean. V., 1981, A Short Title Catalogue of Household and Cookery Books published in the English Tongue 1701–1800, London, pp. 151, 15, 30.

6 Clifford, J.L., ed., 1947, Dr Campbell's Diary of a Visit to England in 1775, Cambridge, p. 50.

7 Hickey, W., Memoirs, vol. ii, 315, quoted in Castro, P., A Dictionary of London Taverns, London Guildhall Ms 3110/2.

8 Targett, P., 1998, Richard Johnson or John Farley?, Petits Propos Culinaires 58, London.

9 Haly, A., ed., 1988, Farley, J., The London Art of Cookery, Southover Press, p. 20.

10 Anon., op. cit., 1768, p. 5.

11 Newnham Davis, Lt.-Col., 1899, Dinners and Diners and How to Dine in London, London, p. 10; the pudding contained a rich mixture of steak and kidney, oysters and larks.

12 Thale, M., ed., 1972, The Autobiography of Francis Place (1771–1854), Cambridge, p. 102; at this

time Place was earning 14s a week.

13 Anon, 1750, 'The London al-n's taste, or pretty Sally of the chop-house', London Guildhall, 1808.

14 Clarke, P., 1983, The English Ale House A Social History 1200–1830, London and New York, p. 210; regional beers could cost 100–200% more than ordinary beers.

15 Earle, P., 1994, A City Full of People, London, p. 145.

16 Anon., 1764, Low-Life: Or One Half of the World Knows not how The Other Half Live, London, p. 93.

17 Anon., op. cit., 1764, p. 56.

18 Smollett, T., 1748, Roderick Random, quoted in Dodd, G., 1856, The Food of London, London, pp. 98–9.

19 Mare, M.L., and Quarrel, W. H., 1938, Lichtenberg's Visits to England, Oxford, pp. 63–4.

20 PRO, PROB.35/5; Inventory of Thomas Carter, Confectioner, St Bride's, 1736, London,

21 The references to chocolate drops and cardamom-flavoured comfits are both early instances of these types of confectionery, which were better known later in the century; personal communication, Ivan Day.

22 Mortimer, 1763, The Universal Director, London, p. 28.

23 CLRO, MISC. Mss/70/2.

24 Brown, P. B., and Day, I., 1997, Pleasures of the Table, York Civic Trust, p. 72.

25 Glasse, H., 1751, The Art of Cookery Made Plain and Easy, 4th edn, London, p. 331.

26 Armitage, P., and McCarthy, L. 1980, 'Turtle Remains from a late 18th Century Well at Leadenhall Buildings', London Archaeology, Winter 1980, vol. 4, no. 1.

27 Samuel Birch & Lucas Birch & Company, 'Day Book, 1775–8', London, Guildhall, Ms 458.

28 Anon., op. cit., 1768, p. 10.

29 Hamlyn, P., ed., 1984, Larousse Gastronomique, London, p. 883.

30 Anon., c.1770, 'Mr Horton's Soup Room', London, Guildhall, 1825.

31 Brillat-Savarin, J.-A., 1825, The Physiology of Taste, London, 1994, pp. 267ff.

32 Britton, J., 1850, Autobiography of John Britton, vol. I, London, p. 83.

33 Timbs, J., 1872, Clubs and Club Life in London, London, pp. 171–2; the meal included a hot apple pie stuck with bay leaves to celebrate Mrs Lennox's debut as an author.

34 Coke, D., 1984, 'Vauxhall Gardens', in Rococo Art and Design in Hogarth's England, Victoria and Albert Museum, pp. 77–8.

35 Wroth, W., 1896, The London Pleasure Gardens of the Eighteenth Century, London, pp. 298–9 for a bill of provisions from 1762.

36 The Wits Magazine, June 1784, Vauxhall Gardens Scrapbook, vol. IV, Museum of London, 61.61/4.

37 Sands, M., 1946, Invitation to Ranelagh, London, p. 133.

38 Smollett, T., 1771, The Expedition of Humphry Clinker, Wordsworth Editions Ltd, 1995, p. 81.

39 Wroth, op. cit., 1898, p. 131.

40 The Connoisseur, 6 July 1764, letter from 'Goliah English', pp. 151–3, p. 151.

41 The Roast Beef of Old England, undated, London, unpaginated.

42 Bindman, D., 1989, The Shadow of the Guillotine, London, p. 127.

The 19th Century

1 Hayward, A., 1883 (1st ed. 1852), The Art of

Dining: or Gastronomy and Gastronomers, London.
2 Hayward, op. cit., 1883, pp. 91–2: for whitebait dinners see Mars, V., 1997, 'Little Fish and Large Appetites. Victorian Whitebait Dinners at Blackwall, Gravesend and Greenwich', in 'Fish from the Waters', *Proceedings of the Oxford Symposium on Food and Cookery*, Prospect Books, pp. 210–9.
3 Jerrold, W.B., 1868, *The Epicure's Year Book and Table Companion*, London, preface, p. v and table of contents.
4 Anon., 1815, *The Epicure's Almanack, or Calendar of Good Living*, London.
5 Anon., op. cit., 1815, p. 133.
6 Anon., op. cit., 1815, pp. 24–5, and Evans, D.M., 1852, *City Men and City Manners*, London, pp. 145–7, and chap. ix for City coffee houses.
7 Anon., op. cit., 1815, p. 6.
8 Dodd, G., 1856, *The Food of London*, London, pp. 506–8.
9 In 1854 Francatelli was paid 300 gn. p.a. as the *chef de cuisine* of the Reform Club; the second cook was paid £150 p.a.; personal communication, Simon Blundell.
10 Adburgham, A., 1983, *Silver Fork Society Fashionable Life and Literature from 1814–1840*, London, p. 263.
11 Ude, L.E., 1819, *The French Cook; or, the Art of Cookery*, London, pp. xviii–xix.
12 *The Builder*, 1846, pp. 340–4.
13 Jerrold, op. cit., 1868, p. 145.
14 Soyer, A., 1846, *The Gastronomic Regenerator*, London.
15 'Coffee Room Complaints and Answers, 1837–42', Reform Club, entry for 27 July 1839.
16 Dodd, op. cit., 1856, pp. 513–4.
17 *Illustrated London News*, 11 July 1846, pp. 17–8.
18 'List of Subscribers to A. Soyer's Plan of the Reform Kitchen & Cookery Book, 1843–1844', Reform Club, Thomas Holt, entry dated 24 November 1846.
19 Jerrold, op. cit., 1868, pp. 2 and 10.
20 Soyer, A., 1848, *Soyer's Charitable Cookery; or, the Poor Man's Regenerator*, London and Dublin.
21 Soyer, op. cit., 1848, p. 15.
22 *The Illustrated Times*, 18 December 1858, p. 402.
23 Jerrold, op. cit., 1868, p. 4.
24 Sala, G.A., 1859, *Twice Around the Clock*, London, pp. 225ff; Sala was described by Edward Dallas as the man who 'probably knows more about the history of cookery in all countries of the world than any man alive' (Dallas, E.S., 1877, *Kettner's Book of the Table*, dedication; new ed. London, 1968).
25 Sala, op.cit., 1859, pp. 265–6.
26 Gissing, G., 1880, *Workers in the Dawn*, part 1, chap. 1, www.lang.nagoya-u.ac.jp/~matsuoka/GG-Dawn-1.
27 Dodd, op. cit., 1856, pp. 514–5.
28 George, D., 1992, *London Life in the Eighteenth Century*, London, pp. 296–7.
29 Smollett, op. cit., 1771, *Humphry Clinker*, p. 111; see also Farley, in Haly, op. cit., 1988, pp. 374–80, 'Considerations on Culinary Poisons & Considerations on the Adulteration of Bread and Flour'.
30 Burnett, J., 1989, *Plenty and Want*, London, pp. 86–103 and 216–39.
31 Allan, A., ed., 1963, *Palace and Hovel or Phases of London Life by Daniel Joseph Kirwan*, 1870, London, New York and Toronto, p. 57.
32 Jerrold, op. cit., 1868, p. 36.
33 For Indian cooking in the 19th century we are grateful for information compiled by MOCHA, the Museum of Culinary History and Alimentation.
34 Glasse, H., 1747, *The Art of Cookery made Plain and Easy*, Prospect Books, 1995, p. 52.
35 *The Times*, 27 March 1811.
36 Fisher, M.H., 1997, *The Travels of Dean Mahomet*, Berkeley and Los Angeles, California.
37 Anon., op. cit., 1815, pp. 123–4.
38 Terry, R., 1861, *Indian Cookery*, London, 1998.
39 'A Catalogue [for the Sale of the] Royal Gardens Vauxhall, August 29 1859', lots 110–2, Vauxhall Gardens Scrapbook, vol. II, Museum of London, 61.61/2.
40 *The Citizen*, 3 August 1889, Savoy Group Archive, PRMa/1.
41 Bacchus & Cordon Bleu, 1885, *New Guide for the Hotel, Bar and Restaurant, Butler and Chef*, London, p. 85.
42 Anon., op. cit., 1815; the *Epicure's Almanack* describes a number of confectioners and pastrycooks frequented by women and states that Farrance's Pastry Shop, Spring Gardens, and Barker's Repository of Confectionery, 106 Bond Street, were particularly popular.
43 *London at Dinner, Where to Dine in 1858*, facsimile published by David & Charles, 1969; p. 11; the first ed. was published in 1851.
44 Bliss, T., ed., 1949, *Jane Welsh Carlyle: A New Selection of her Letters*, pp. 233–4, 10 August 1852.
45 *London at Dinner*, op. cit., p. 11.
46 Anon., op. cit., 1815, Guedon's, p. 144: Four Nations kept by M. Barron, pp. 150–1; Huntly's Coffee House and Tavern directed by M. Chedron, p. 152.
47 Simpson's is described as 'John Simpson's Grand Restauratum' in a newspaper advertisement quoted by Lt.-Col. Newnham-Davis in a booklet on Simpson's in the Strand, undated but c.1910, p. 1.
48 Sala, op. cit., 1859, p. 142.
49 Pascoe, C.E., 1893, *London of Today*, London, p. 86, and chap. 5 for dining in London.
50 Thorne, R., 1980, 'Places of Refreshment in the nineteenth-century City', in *Buildings & Society: essays on the social development of the built environment*, King, A.D., ed., p. 239.
51 An advertisement for the St James's Restaurant in Piccadilly which highlights ladies' retiring rooms and lavatories suggests that these facilities were still uncommon ten years later, see, *London A Complete Guide to the Places of Amusement*, 1877, London, pp. 174ff.
52 For a comprehensive survey of restaurants at the end of the century see, Newnham-Davis, Lt.-Col., 1899, *Dinners and Diners and How to Dine in London*, London.
53 Simmons, J., 1968, *St Pancras Station*, London, pp. 56–8, 80–1.
54 Sanderson, J.M., 1870, *The Langham Hotel Guide to London*, London, p. 5.
55 The American Bar was installed in 1898. From 1903–24 it was run by Ada Coleman, who invented the 'Hanky Panky'. Savoy Group Archive SBs/COLEMAN &Ja/4/260.
56 *Illustrated Sporting and Dramatic News*, 1 November 1890, Savoy Group Archive, PRMa/1.
57 For an early example of a waiter carving on a side-table (at the Blue Posts, Cork Street), see, *London at Dinner*, op. cit., p. 9.

The 20th Century

1 *Evening Standard*, 14 April 1999, reporting a recent London Research Centre survey into London lifestyles.
2 George, W.L., 1921, *A London Mosaic*, London, p. 65.
3 Burke, T., 1934, *London in my Time*, London, p. 33.
4 The list is derived from various sources, see in particular chap. 5 'Restaurants of the Nations' in *Where to Dine in London*, by 'Bon Viveur' (Christopher Wentworth Dilke), 1937.
5 Scott, C., probably 1896, *Souvenir of the Trocadero*, London, unpaginated.
6 Burke, op. cit., 1934, p. 177.
7 Ward Lock & Co., 1908, *Guide to London*, London, p. xxvii.
8 Machray, R., 1902, *The Night Side of London*, London, pp. 69–70.
9 Burke, T., 1919, *Out and About*, London, p. 50.
10 See Cork, R.,1985, *Art Beyond the Gallery in early 20th-century England*, New Haven and London, chap.5, pp. 214–47, 'The Restaurant de la Tour Eiffel'.
11 Burke, op. cit., 1934, p. 185.
12 Jackson, S., 1947, *An Indiscreet Guide to Soho*, London, p. 68.
13 Burke, op. cit., 1934, p. 174.
14 Burke, op. cit., 1934, p. 32.
15 See Parkin, M.,1981, *A Salute to Marcel Boulestin & Jean-Emile Laboureur*, London.
16 Burke, op. cit., 1934, pp. 178–9.
17 Hooten-Smith, E., 1928, *The Restaurants of London*, London, has a short chapter on Sandys, pp. 152–4.
18 Promotional leaflet for the Black And White Milk Bar, undated, Museum of London.
19 Newnham-Davis, N., 1914, *The Gourmet's Guide to London*, London, p. 77.
20 Newnham-Davis, N., 1899, *Dinners and Diners and How to Dine in London*, London, p. 94.
21 Burke, T., 1915, *Nights in Town*, London, p. 280. He is describing Jumbo's eating house in Homerton.
22 Pember Reeves, M., 1913, *Round About a Pound a Week*, London.
23 Spring Rice, M., 1939, *Working-Class Wives*, London, p. 201.
24 Houston Bowden, G., 1975, *British Gastronomy*, London, p. 83. Most of the details in this paragraph are taken from this source.
25 Houston Bowden, op. cit., 1975, p. 88, claims the first was opened in a basement of the Harrington Hotel.
26 Baynes, K. and K., 'Eating Out can be Fun', *Design*, February 1966, p. 35.
27 *Evening Standard*, Friday 9 June 1975, p. 45, 'The McDonald's Recipie for Profit'.
28 Jackson, S., op. cit., 1947, p. 84.
29 Jackson, S., op. cit., 1947, p. 86. The other quotes in this paragraph are from restaurant advertisements in the front of this book.

Focus

30 Dunn-Meynell, H., 1985, 'The Five Shilling Meal', *International Wine & Good Food Society*, p. 166

List of abbreviations

CLRO	Corporation of London Record Office
EETS	Early English Text Society
G. Lib.	Guidhall Library, London
OED	Oxford English Dictionary
PRO	Public Record Office, London

Index